Achieving and Sustaining Secured Business Operations

An Executive's Guide to Planning and Management

Neelesh Ajmani
Dinesh Kumar

Apress®

Achieving and Sustaining Secured Business Operations: An Executive's Guide to Planning and Management

Neelesh Ajmani
Hopkinton, Massachusetts, USA

Dinesh Kumar
Chadds Ford, Pennsylvania, USA

ISBN-13 (pbk): 978-1-4842-3098-5
https://doi.org/10.1007/978-1-4842-3099-2

ISBN-13 (electronic): 978-1-4842-3099-2

Library of Congress Control Number: 2017961550

Cover image designed by Freepik

Managing Director: Welmoed Spahr
Editorial Director: Todd Green
Acquisitions Editor: Susan McDermott
Development Editor: Laura Berendson
Technical Reviewer: Rajesh Sukumaran
Coordinating Editor: Rita Fernando
Copy Editor: Karen Jameson

Distributed to the book trade worldwide by Springer Science+Business Media New York, 233 Spring Street, 6th Floor, New York, NY 10013. Phone 1-800-SPRINGER, fax (201) 348-4505, e-mail orders-ny@springer-sbm.com, or visit www.springeronline.com. Apress Media, LLC is a California LLC and the sole member (owner) is Springer Science + Business Media Finance Inc (SSBM Finance Inc). SSBM Finance Inc is a **Delaware** corporation.

For information on translations, please e-mail rights@apress.com, or visit http://www.apress.com/rights-permissions.

Apress titles may be purchased in bulk for academic, corporate, or promotional use. eBook versions and licenses are also available for most titles. For more information, reference our Print and eBook Bulk Sales web page at http://www.apress.com/bulk-sales.

Any source code or other supplementary material referenced by the author in this book is available to readers on GitHub via the book's product page, located at www.apress.com/9781484230985. For more detailed information, please visit http://www.apress.com/source-code.

Printed on acid-free paper

Table of Contents

About the Authors

 **Neelesh Ajmani** has over 28 years of experience in solving critical business issues in public and private sectors with expertise in digital transformation, risk management, secured business operations, strategic planning, organizational design, agile program management, enterprise architecture and information management. Neelesh is a Program Management Specialist Advisor in the Health Care and Life Sciences Industry practice of NTT Data Services. In affiliation with Mitovia, Inc., as Chief Services Officer, he is advising and developing the body of knowledge and services offerings for achieving and sustaining secured business operations. In the past, Neelesh worked at Cisco for 15 years in advisory, delivery, and leadership roles, specializing in Internet Commerce, Identity and Access Management, and Manufacturing solutions. Neelesh has delivered business solutions with the state-of-the art technology solutions for many Fortune 500 organizations in Manufacturing, Banking industries, Supreme Court of India, and federal government of India. He has an MBA from San Jose State University, and an MS in Computer Applications from Jawaharlal Nehru University, India. Neelesh is certified in Advanced Program Management from Stanford University, PMP, TOGAF Enterprise Architecture, and is an ITIL V3 Expert.

Connect with Neelesh at linkedin.com/in/neeleshajmani or at neelesh.ajmani@gmail.com

Dinesh Kumar is Cofounder and CTO at Mitovia, has over 30 years of experience in technology business management, strategic planning, value measurement and communication, capability assessment and planning, and governance. At Mitovia he is driving business-minded, knowledge-driven practices and solutions for planning and managing organizational capabilities, including digital, security, competency, and shared services management. Dinesh has filed a patent on capability-driven, service-oriented planning. He is also an adjunct professor at Stevens Institute of Technology, teaching technology business management and process innovation courses to MBA and MSIS students. Dinesh is a board member and principal at the Innovation Value Institute, where he is developing and driving capability models and practices for managing IT for business value. He is a founding member and major contributor at The Value Council, a nonprofit organization focused on improving value management practices. Previously Dinesh has held a broad variety of sales, consulting, and management roles at Microsoft, Informix, and Unisys. He has an MBA degree from Penn State University and an MS in Computer Science from Rutgers University.

Connect with Dinesh at linkedin.com/in/dineshku or dineshk@mitovia.com

About the Technical Reviewer

Rajesh Sukumaran has over 19 years of experience in various technology domains with proven technical leadership and management skills. Rajesh has been working as a security professional for over a decade in designing, architecting, and deploying Identity and Access Management solutions, Security Risk analysis, Compliance and Auditing technologies, Single Sign on, Federated Identity, Enterprise System Architecture, Authentication and Authorization technologies, Strategy and Governance, and custom-built security frameworks. Rajesh is a Certified Information Systems Security Professional (CISSP) and he is currently working as a Security Systems Specialist Advisor at NTT Data Services. He leads the Security Services division focusing on IAM architecture, leading enterprise security and drive profitable growth and innovative thinking. In the past, he has played many roles as security architect, technical manager, database administrator, and data warehouse specialist. Rajesh has a Masters in computer applications from University of Kerala, India. He is currently focused on Risk-based Identity Intelligence, IoT (Internet of Things) security and cloud security solutions.

Connect with Rajesh at https://www.linkedin.com/in/rajesh-sukumaran-cissp-43a6236/ or psrajesh@gmail.com

Acknowledgments

This book is truly a product of years of learnings, observations, experiences, support, and encouragement. Many people have directly helped, guided, and impacted us, and many more did in a subtle, maybe in a subconscious way. Thank you.

The journey of writing the book would not have started without Paul Rohmeyer, Security Expert and Professor at Stevens Institute of Technology; and Susan McDermott, Editor at Apress. Paul established a Financial Cyber Security lab at the university, and he invited us to present our work on secured business operations at its first conference in 2016. Susan found the topic interesting and refreshing and asked us to write a book. Thank you, Paul and Susan, for the opportunities to share our work and inspiration to write this book.

Special thanks to Rita Fernando at Apress for keeping us motivated and on track, and Rajesh Sukumaran at NTT Data Services for lending us the domain knowledge and reviewing the complete manuscript.

Personal note from Neelesh

I would like to thank Arun Saxena at HCL; Brenda Bernal Hughes at Symantec; Charles Li at Shell; David Clingan, Nitin Keskar, and Tim Dries at Cisco; Jeff Tri at Mayo Clinic; Katrina Doerfler at Amazon; Krisnakumar Narayanan (KK) at Dell EMC; Nasrin Rezai at GE; and Vijay Bhatt at Harvard Pilgrim Health Care, who were mentors and colleagues at various stages of my professional life. They helped to shape my perspective on developing a holistic and structured framework for managing cybersecurity; solving this problem holistically by focusing on top-down and bottom-up perspectives. I am glad and thankful to Rajesh Sukumuran, my colleague and security expert at NTT Data Services for graciously accepting to be the technical reviewer of this book. The gratitude goes to my spouse, Mukta, who supported all along in this journey and motivated me spiritually and emotionally to fulfill this dream.

Personal note from Dinesh

In writing this book, I realized more than ever how important family is in getting where you want to be. I am grateful to my wife, Rashmi, for her unconditional sacrifices, reviewing, and providing feedback throughout the process; to my daughters, Niketa and Trisha, for being my therapists at times, teaching me color aesthetics, and keeping things simple.

Professionally, I would like to thank my believers, customers, partners, and colleagues for providing the opportunities and environment to pursue my vision and passion. Particularly, Paul Rohmeyer at Stevens Institute of Technology; Jeanne Ross and Peter Weill at CISR, MIT; Earl Newsome at Estee Lauder (now at Praxair); Larry Alonso at Estee Lauder; Jordon Corn at AAA; Clark Brown at Esterline; Jame Healy at Alescent; Martin Curley at Intel (now at Mastercard); Jim Kenneally at Intel; Jack Anderson at Chevron; Charles Wallace at Rohm and Haas (now at Solenis); John Holmes at Rathbeau Technologies; Jim Boots at Chevron; Mushir Din at Compugen (now at Vitalgrid); Rich Burton and Dan Garlewicz at Core Systems Group; Jon Erikson at Forrester; Sue Pallini, Nitin Bhatia, Tom Koedding, Don Koscheka, Kristin Kinan and Rick Merrifield at Microsoft; Juan Manuel Santos Rodriguez at Microsoft (now at Citrix); Giuseppe Mascarella at Value Amplify; Tari Schreider at Vitalgrid; Shimon Abouzaglo and Jack Keen at The Value Council; Sharad Joshi and Sridhar Kumaravelu at DTCC; Matt Craig at BNY Mellon; Carl Dister at ReliabilityFirst; Martin Delaney, Declan Kavanagh and Conor O'Brien at IVI; Atul Agrawal at OCTalk; Gordon Butte at Decision Partners; David Pultorak, and Sriram Sabesan – for indulging in countless thought-provoking conversations, and shaping many of the concepts in the book and beyond.

I would also like to acknowledge the support and commitment of my coauthor, Neelesh, for his disciplined and pragmatic approach to incorporating different points of views in our writing. I couldn't even imagine the finish line without him.

Introduction

"Every security services or technology provider tells me all the things I must have. They don't tell me what makes sense for my mission to have," said the program manager of one of the missions at the U.S. Navy. This comment highlights the pain and the challenges that we have seen with planning and managing of security across organizations. The growing pains, bottom-up approach, lack of business ownership and accountability, and technology-driven security industry - motivated us to develop the management model and write this book. A great deal of research, frameworks, and supporting documentation are available on the topic of cybersecurity from government and semi-government entities, academic institutions, and professional organizations across the globe. Not surprisingly, most literature is grounded on governance, risk management, compliance, and operational controls. So, when we began to write, we started by asking, how do we address the concern of the program manager at the U.S. Navy and others who want the right security posture with the right cost, risk, and value.

For more than 15 years, we have been developing and using capability models to bridge the gap between business and IT, assess the current and defined desired state, understand dependencies, prioritize and develop road maps, and monitor progress. We have applied these models for digital transformation, cloud readiness, service management, business process improvements, and many other business and IT initiatives. For most of our careers, we have also been part of many client engagements, delivering infrastructure and security assessments, architecture strategies, business cases, governance, and solution designs. Based on experience across business and IT, strategy and operations, and capabilities and technologies, it was obvious we needed a capability framework.

Although there exists a large body of knowledge about security practices, we couldn't find a model that does the following:

- speaks the language of the business,

- focuses on enabling business outcomes,

- supports a variety of organizations and business models,

- is actionable.

Thus, we embarked on a mission of organizing, formalizing, and extending our learnings into a business-centric capability framework for achieving and sustaining secured business operations. For quite some time, we had been using/refining the model in our business engagements; it was publicly launched at the Financial Cyber Security conference at Stevens Institute of Technology in 2016. Soon after, this book was conceived.

Throughout the framework design and development of the book, we have kept our focus on the following guiding principles:

1. People are driven by their needs. The body of knowledge must be comprehensive, yet contextual and useful for people in business and IT.

2. People can only evaluate what they observe, and plan what they know. The characteristics and practices at each capability maturity level must be observable.

3. Achieving the highest maturity level may not be the best value for an organization. The maturity model must be designed as a road map to value.

4. Some things must change to create value. Organizations must be able to operationalize the model with a purpose-built management platform for assessment, planning, and ongoing monitoring.

5. Start anywhere, go everywhere. Security is a broad
    and complex capability with dependencies to many
    other capabilities. Organizations may use the model
    top down, bottom up, or middle out.

These principles have helped us deliver a practical framework and
structure this book for business and IT management, architects, service
owners, and providers.

The body of knowledge is presented in seven chapters in the book.
Logically, the chapters follow a classic strategy to execution methodology
of why, what, and how. If you are a businessperson, you may start with
the first three chapters, followed by Chapters 6 and 7. Then, turn your
attention to the remaining Chapters 4 and 5, which focus on operational
and management capabilities and practices for secured business
operations.

The first chapter provides an assessment of the current state of the
security industry and prevailing practices. It concludes that current
practices are insufficient in achieving and sustaining secured business
operations. The breadth and depth of security practices are of no value
if they don't enable business to do what business wants to do safely and
securely.

The second chapter articulates the vision and opportunity for an
organization to leverage security as a competitive advantage. It introduces
next practices for business-driven security capability management,
starting with a business engagement model for identifying the required
risk-resilience level for the organization. Security is not a one-size-fits-all
capability. To avoid overinvesting or underinvesting in security capabilities
it is important for organizations to know the extent of business interactions
and the associated risks. As you read the chapter, you might be able
to determine the engagement model and risk-resilience level of your
organization.

The next three chapters, Chapters 3-5, take you inside the body of the framework for achieving and sustaining secured business operations.

The third chapter is about the business perspective on secured business operations. The secured business model, described in this chapter, introduces five performance domains (5 Ps) - Prevent, Protect, Profile, Policy, and People. These 5 Ps allow business leaders to understand, communicate, and manage the security needs based on the business drivers and risk resilience required for the level of business engagement. A clear understanding of the business risk and required business capabilities provides a prescriptive guidance to business and IT operations, ensures end-to-end alignment, and drives business accountability for achieving and sustaining secured business operations.

In the fourth chapter, we get into the guts of what it will take to secure business operations at the desired level of risk resilience. It explains the secured operating model of the framework, addressing twenty-one operational capabilities organized into six capability domains. The six capability domains are - Business Management, Operations Management, Risk Management, Compliance Controls, Master Data Management, and Infrastructure Management. The secured operating model provides the management bridge between business needs as defined by the secured business model and various operational practices and technical solutions required, implemented, and suggested by many security, risk, and compliance frameworks. For people in the trenches who are responsible for day-to-day security operations, an assessment using the secured operating model can help them understand how well the operational capabilities are aligned with business needs, address the gaps, and show value of their efforts. On the other hand, the management can evaluate the current state, identify the gap, prioritize what must be done, and monitor progress against the plan.

In the fifth chapter, we describe the secured management model for creating the discipline and culture of ensuring secured business operations by design. Planning and implementing security is everyone's job.

Any change created by any project must have appropriate security measures. Therefore, we have included a methodology to help organizations operationalize the security mindset in every business/IT project or initiative. The management model defines inputs, outputs, and key activities across the life cycle of assessing, planning, improving, and managing capabilities and solutions. The management practices in this model are critical for sustaining secured business operations.

The sixth chapter describes key performance indicators (KPIs) and methods for measuring effectiveness of security capabilities and efforts. Most organizations have activity-based measures for compliance reporting. Constantly, business leaders ask - are we doing the right thing? Are we producing the desired outcomes? How do we know? Measuring and ensuring effectiveness requires going beyond the activity-based KPIs. It requires understanding how value flows from solutions to outcomes. The chapter introduces techniques for creating a value flow map and measuring value contribution along the way, knowing that security effectiveness is key to overcoming planning by fear. It drives accountability and effective decision making at all levels in the organization. Alignment and measurement are core to the framework, and therefore, they are described in Chapter 6.

The seventh chapter is a takeaway chapter. It includes key learnings from the previous six chapters. The chapter also includes a few use cases, how other organizations have used various aspects of the framework. Last, it includes a set of recommendations on adopting the framework and overcoming barriers and constraints in your organization.

Feedback and Follow-Up

We know we are not there yet, and we realize, there is always a next maturity level to strive for, next practice to develop. As we make further strides, we would like to collaborate with you in continuing this journey. We are very keen to hear - what do you like about the framework and the book? What can or should be revised or presented differently? What have you done and what do you intend to do with the framework? Would you like to assess your organization using the framework? You can connect with us on LinkedIn, through email, or at securedbusinessops.com website.

Neelesh Ajmani
Dinesh Kumar

CHAPTER 1

Current Practices

The world is well connected and discoverable for both good and bad people. Throwing money at the problem may only compound the problem.

Information Security, a Growth Industry?

There is hardly a day when information security is not occupying one of the top slots in the newswire. Each time there is a piece of bad news or a security outbreak, organizations are quick to announce initiatives related to information security, cybersecurity, hacking, malware, data loss prevention (DLP), personal data, identity, and access management. Numerous organizations have been increasingly spending millions of dollars on such initiatives and still not getting any relief from cybercrimes and data breaches. Cybersecurity has become a high-growth industry with a predicted 9.8% yearly compound annual growth rate (CAGR) between 2015–2020.[1] The global spending on IT security was at $75.5B in 2015, expected to be $101B by 2018, and will likely reach $170B by 2020. A significant proportion of this spending is allocated to fraud and data breach detection with emphasis on Security Analytics, Threat Intelligence, Mobile Security, and Cloud Security.

---

[1]Gartner Group, IDC, British Lloyds.

© Neelesh Ajmani and Dinesh Kumar 2017
N. Ajmani and D. Kumar, *Achieving and Sustaining Secured Business Operations*,
https://doi.org/10.1007/978-1-4842-3099-2_1

The irony is that Cybersecurity has become an industry, a growth industry. As it produces goods (software, hardware) and related services within an economy, from technical benchmarks, it does meet the definition of an industry. Since the Industrial Revolution, industries have been created to improve the standard of living and to foster the growth of a country or a global region. The security industry is growing as it has become a mandatory expense to work and live in the connected and interdependent world. The Information and Internet have many positive outcomes, connecting people, processes, and organizations around the world; creating millions of jobs; and adding trillions of dollars in the global economies. Chief among the recent innovations include the Internet of Things, Digitization, Social Media, Mobile, and Big Data; these are collectively transforming the organizational culture and lifestyle of the people. Personal identities to all owned assets at every level have either already been converted to digital forms, or are in the process of being converted to a digital form. The business processes are being digitized for better transparency and agility. As an individual or as an organization, a connected and transparent world is a blessing and a curse. How does a growing investment in information security help you effectively manage the potential vulnerabilities while being innovative in products and processes, connected and collaborative with customers and partners, and open to work from anywhere? Can you afford to continue to spend more money?

State of the Business

As per the world economic forum, cybersecurity is costing businesses $400B–$500B in damages per year. Much more damage is not reported due to lack of appropriate understanding and quantification of impact, compliance, or reporting regulations.

Understandably, board of directors or management officials do not want to see the name of their organization in the news about a security breach. What has surprised us is how these very people act in managing security protocols and how they react when things go wrong. Whenever a high-profile incident takes place, the board of directors seeks information from the management, particularly the CIO or head of IT, about potential exposure. In most cases, they simply don't want to be surprised and need assurance that IT is taking all the necessary precautions to avoid unwanted publicity. During regular board meetings, security becomes just another line item limited to status updates regarding security initiatives and measures that IT has taken since the previous review.

We know that senior leadership and line managers have many agendas on their plates that preoccupy their time and attention – competing in the marketplace, monitoring business results, and driving improvements in their area of control. Business is frequently quite clear and direct in what business wants IT to do in terms of new capabilities or improvement in systems. When it comes to security, they tend to take a reactionary approach by leaving it up to the CIO and the IT team to figure out the strategy and technology solutions for managing threats, fraud, and breach detection. Even in case of compliance, for example, PCI or Sox, business tends to focus on them from a technical point of view, thus expecting IT to take care of the compliance requirements. The funding for security projects is generally sourced and approved generously due to fears of cybercrime or compliance exposure.

State of the Security Practices

The IT group is responsible for managing technology solutions used by the business. As many of the applications are purchased rather than developed in-house, the security focus has been on the infrastructure, for example, controlling devices, limiting access, monitoring traffic, detecting fraud and policy violations.

As information security management is delegated to the IT department, the security industry has been primarily focused on developing frameworks and solutions for managing information security by managing infrastructure security.

The wide range of security standards, guidelines, and controls are available from the National Institute of Standards and Technology (NIST), Department of Energy and Department of Homeland Security (DHS), International Organization for Standardization (ISO), and Center for Internet Security (CIS) Organization. The following table provides a high-level summary of the purpose and intent of these frameworks and practices. Table 1-1 provides a quick summary of these frameworks. Check out online the web site securedbusinessops.com for additional details on these frameworks.

Table 1-1. *List of Security Frameworks*

Cybersecurity Framework (NIST)
To identify, protect, and detect security vulnerabilities in critical infrastructure, and to respond and recover from security incidents. The critical infrastructure includes systems in organization's property or in the cloud.

Cyber Security Maturity Model (C2M2, Department of Energy and Homeland Security)
A set of practices organized into ten domains to secure Information Technology and Operational Technology assets and the environments in which they operate. It emphasizes end-to-end process management.

ISO 27001 and 27002 (International Organization for Standardization)
The ISO 2700x series of standards, guidelines, and associated certifications are very extensive in nature and are the greatest source of details for IT to develop Information Security Management Systems. They emphasize implementation of controls for managing information risk.

Center for Internet Security (CIS)
Twenty security controls for addressing cyber risks. These controls address the areas that could pose cyber threats. These controls are being referenced by many other frameworks such as NIST and HIPAA, and used by organizations investigating Internet security threats and data breaches.

There are many other public, nonprofit, and commercial organizations that have developed methodologies and tools to prevent unauthorized access, detect vulnerabilities and incidents, and restore the service in case of a disruption. Most of them view security as a technical problem requiring a technical solution.

Anything Wrong with the Current State?

Nothing is wrong with technology solutions and practices, which are designed to address security challenges. Truly! The solutions and practices exist because there is a market for such products and services. What may be wrong is our mindset, our attitude, or our approach to planning and managing security. We find them quite like many transformative paradigms and revolutionized IT decisions in the past decades, such as Quality in 1980s, Automation in 1990s, Internet in 2000s, and Digital in 2010s.

Considering Quality, Automation, Internet and Digital have direct connection with customers and products, so one would think that business management would take a keener interest and ownership in driving, shaping, and exploiting them for business advantage. Eventually, Business did but it didn't start that way. Initially, Quality was viewed as a manufacturing problem, thus it was left to the manufacturing plants to figure out what they could do to improve quality. Management considered quality as a cost of being in the business and a necessity for being competitive. Even after spending millions of dollars in designing and implementing quality processes, and auditing quality, many companies failed to create a quality culture and a sustainable quality advantage. Successful organizations transformed the business model and business strategy based on quality as a competitive differentiation. These organizations have realized the challenges for organizations to continuously produce or deliver quality products and services while simultaneously reducing the cost. Accordingly, they started managing quality as a differentiating organizational capability, posturing quality as a value driver, not as a cost to the business.

Technology has triggered many business innovations. For example, the Internet has provided global access and reduced barrier to entry and Digital technologies have enabled real-time access. It may seem obvious for business management to delegate planning and delivery of technology-based innovation to the technology group. At the same time, it is also obvious that most organizations are not being able to fully realize the potential of technology innovations. The reason is quite simple – technology alone does not create the desired change in the organization, and surely does not provide a sustainable advantage. The business management who understood and integrated technology-enabled innovation into business planning and governance enjoyed the trajectory of continued growth and highly satisfied customers, partners, and employees. If you have not already, you may want to find out – how many technologies have your organization purchased that have never been deployed? What percentage of employees has changed their workplace behaviors in response to a new technology solution? Are you surprised with your findings? What is the root cause of whatever you found?

What's wrong with the current security frameworks and practices is exactly what has been ailing many of the past practices in addressing organizational challenges and transformation initiatives. Could you have improved and sustained sales growth just by implementing a customer relationship management (CRM) system without having the appropriate skills, staffing, culture, and processes? Could you have sustained customer loyalty just by implementing big data and social connections without having the customer-centric product design, development, and support? Can you avoid cost and realize the business value of IT just by outsourcing or going to the cloud? Can you be safe and secure just by building technological walls and barriers? Ask yourself and people around you, how current practices and management attitude are making us innovative and responsive while being safe and secure?

Transforming Fear Into Confidence and Advantage

Rather than asking what IT is doing to protect the business, the business should be asking what are they doing to run business operations uninterrupted, safe, and secure. Rather than viewing monies spent on information security as a necessary expense, organizations should be considering information security as a strategic differentiation. Information security is a business-critical issue. The fear of potential failure can't be left up to the technology savvy people of the company to address with the notion that technology created this problem and only technology can solve it. The fear needs to be transformed into confidence that creates business value by embracing the challenge. The question is not, is security a business or technology problem? It is business critical to gain customer confidence, workforce confidence, grow the business, increase competitiveness, gain market share, improve productivity, and socially contribute to improve the living standards of the society. Security is not a technology problem; rather, it is impacting all the business drivers directly. Security should be tamed with confidence to improve business operations overall with the proactive approaches and not reactionary with fear. Ultimately, securing business operations will generate sustainable business value.

To get different results, we need to do things differently. We need new practices where we look at and manage security business down, not just technology up. Individual and technology accountabilities are not sufficient. It requires cross-functional decisions and collaboration for end-to-end securing of business operations.

The next chapter introduces the framework and a set of next practices for transforming the management approach and managing the organizational capabilities for achieving and sustaining secured business operations.

CHAPTER 2

Next Practices: Business-Centric Security and Risk Management

Manage security as an organizational capability, not as a liability. For sustained competitive advantage, an organization must consider security their friend, not a foe.

Business State

Regardless of the industry and size of the organization, there is a fundamental shift within every business and operating model. Organizations are dependent on each other, requiring a much tighter, integrated, and timely flow of information. The type of information and with whom they share information will only expand with time. In the online world, everything is a service and is fast becoming a self-service. Organizations can no longer function in isolation.

© Neelesh Ajmani and Dinesh Kumar 2017
N. Ajmani and D. Kumar, *Achieving and Sustaining Secured Business Operations*,
https://doi.org/10.1007/978-1-4842-3099-2_2

The organizations will continue to push the envelope on how technology can help them become more productive, reduce the cost of doing business, provide new and better products and services to their customers and partners, make better and faster decisions, and introduce new business and operating models.

To manage business, leaders are always looking for ways to innovate and drive their competitiveness in the marketplace. They are always asking the IT function to simplify and enhance their capabilities to communicate, collaborate, connect, and consolidate information and transactions across people and processes inside and outside the organization. Organizations like to collect a lot more information about their customers so that they can become more responsive to customers' needs, and thereby, better respond to their needs and promote relevant products and services. Organizations want their customers to self-help themselves through their mobile devices or whatever method they choose. They want to seamlessly integrate or interact with machines, devices, and systems belonging to other people or organizations for a real-time flow of information and actions.

In every organization we have worked with, consistently, it has been found that business management spends lot of time, energy, and money in thinking and managing the capabilities they need to run and grow the business. We have also found that business-initiated projects mostly, if not entirely, are about new business capabilities. The capabilities generally require new roles or new tools of trade. As most of the functionality or capabilities are grounded on digital technologies, unlike wet floors or operating machinery, most organizations don't think their people will get hurt. As a result, the safety and security of information is not often considered in advance or during process or solution engineering. Over the years, the organizations have learned that a rework does not always produce the same quality, controls, and satisfaction even after spending a great amount of time and money. The same is true for information and transactional security in any business process. To overcome the unnecessary spending and associated risks, any business capability planning must include delivery of a secured business capability.

Security as a Competitive Differentiation

A recent report,[1] published by AIG that is based on a study conducted in the United Kingdom shows the following results:

- 45% of companies surveyed have already experienced a cyber security breach.

- 62% believe it likely that their company will suffer an attack within the next 12 months.

- 56% of European data breaches were caused by internal company employees or by other areas internal to the company.

- 52% of companies said they either rarely or never discussed information security in board meetings.

- 36% still designate maintenance of cyber security as an IT department function.

In the previous chapter, we questioned the need for a growing cybersecurity industry. Even with the large sum of money spent on information security infrastructure, organizations continue to fear and experience security breaches because of the low level of maturity in their security management capabilities. It means, if planned and managed right, security can be a major competitive differentiation in the age of digital business where everything is a service.

---

[1]https://www.aig.com/knowledge-and-insights/k-and-i-article-cyber-security-board-level-issue

If you look back, you can clearly see how business management attitude has changed over the last few decades around product and service quality. At the start of global competition, it all began with the need to survive in the marketplace and considered cost of quality as a cost of doing business. Just like the information security industry today, there was a growing industry around total quality management with plenty of methodologies. Many organizations embarked on major transformational, quality initiatives and promoted themselves as quality-first organizations. In spite of these quality initiatives, some organizations could not survive while others were able to create a sustainable competitive advantage with quality as a core differentiating ingredient.[2] This time cybersecurity is no different than quality. Just like quality, security is not one person's or one group's responsibility. It is everyone's responsibility. It takes people, process, information, technology, and culture to do it right and, more importantly, sustain it. If done right and managed right, secured business operations will also be a key contributor to ongoing business advantage. The organizations recognize that product quality is not a difficult subject for business leaders to understand, and therefore they have been willing to commit and proactively drive desired outcomes. For business leaders to see security as a business differentiation rather than a business nuisance, they need to describe and organize it in a business context. Not in terms of their negative impact on the business but in terms of business outcomes. Not as a shiny object but as an integral part of the culture.

---

[2]Hung Chung Su, Kevin Linderman, Roger G. Schroeder, and Andrew H. Van De Ven, **"A Comparative Case Study of Sustaining Quality as a Competitive Advantage,"** *Journal of Operations Management* 32:7-8 (2014): 429–45.

Secured Business Operations, an Organizational Capability

Let's start with a term that is business-centric and clearly articulates the business objective – Secured Business Operations. Cybersecurity may be a mean; the secured business operation is the destination or outcome that will ultimately produce the desired results.

Secured Business Operations is an organizational capability, providing an ongoing ability for protecting information and assets, preventing unauthorized access, ensuring trust and peace of mind, and safeguarding a firm's brand while continuing innovation and delivering differentiating experience and services for its customers, partners, and employees.

Every product or service provided by an organization can be viewed like a coin with two sides. One side represents its value for the consuming organization or an individual; and the other side represents the warranty from the issuer, that is, it can be trusted for using whenever or wherever. Any business operation, whether internally within the organization or externally with other people or organizations, must have the right functional capabilities, that is, fit for purpose to produce the desired outcomes. At the same time, the business operation should also be secured and reliable enough, that is, fit for use for people to trust and participate in the operation. It doesn't matter how good the functional capabilities are if no one is willing to adopt and use them. For sustainable business advantage, every business operation needs to be fit for purpose and fit for use – in other words, it must be a secured business operation.

Now, how secure do the "secured" business operations need to be?

Whenever you talk with technology, process, compliance, or a framework subject-matter expert about securing business, the typical response is in terms of a list of "ideal" practices. Frequently, these experts quote these practices as best practices, not best for you but what has been best for someone else. Many of them also take the mindset of being risk-averse, that is, anything short of the extreme or what is considered the best, has a risk that must be eliminated.

Except in case of life and death or some moral, ethical issues, most of the business decisions are based on return on investment. Any lack of appropriate investment does introduce potential business or financial risk. It should not be about eliminating future potential risk today, it must be about understanding and willingness to accept the potential cost of follow-up actions needed in response to the situation when potential risk is materialized. In the end, good business decisions are based on cost and value of doing something, and not on cost and risk of not doing something. There is no right or wrong answer on what that something is. To adequately answer the question, "how secured your business operations need to be?," you must first identify the appropriate level of risk resilience for your organization. So, rather than getting caught up in the details and frankly in the noise of all the technical opinions, the next framework and practices need to be business-centric by design and must leverage the laws of gravity.

"Where will the apple fall" – can be determined quite easily when we are looking from the top of the tree compared to looking up from the ground and not sure which apple are we focusing on.

A safety and security risk is introduced whenever there is a handshake or distribution of information between two parties. The parties can be individuals, processes, systems, or devices regardless of their location and affiliation with the organization. If the information remains in the sole custody of the source and there are no windows or holes in the walls around the source for someone to peak in, there will not be a cybersecurity industry and we won't be writing this book. As we studied many organizations across industries, we found that the security risk resilience level of the organization can be reasonably evaluated and projected based on the types of interaction with its own employees; between its own functions; and with external people, processes, and

14

organizations. Consider the business engagement model to understand these interactions.

A business engagement model helps you identify the "right" security posture or risk resilience level for the business, and guide the execution trajectory for achieving and sustaining secured business operations, thus avoiding overengineering and ensuring alignment at every level and across the organization.

The model consists of four distinct engagement levels, describing the reach and range of engagement. See Table 2-1 for a summary of the engagement models. The engagement levels are progressive, that is, as the organization grows, it typically extends its ecosystem and capabilities, thus increasing the reach and range of interactions.

Table 2-1. *Business Engagement model*

Level	Archetype	Characteristics
1	Core Business	All business transactions and information are maintained and managed within the confines of the business. No information in digital form is shared outside the walls of the organization.
2	Business to Business	Business regularly performs electronic transactions and shares documents/information with customers and partners.
3	Connected Business	Employees, customers, and partners can access information and conduct business over the Internet.
4	Digital Business	We are a well-integrated and transparent organization, working like a virtual organization with many of our customers and partners.

The business engagement model provides for every planner and decision maker in a business context. It also ensures that downstream security measures and actions support required and desired business activities. With this understanding and alignment, risk and necessary actions needed to manage the risk can be characterized.

At each engagement level, the organization needs to have business capabilities and a competency level in recognizing, analysing, and managing various types of security risks an organization may face. Even if the two organizations are operating at the same engagement level, say connected business, their risk resilience capabilities and competencies may vary. Table 2-2 outlines the summary and structure of a security risk resilience capability map. The subsequent chapters will leverage this map for in-depth assessment and planning of various business and operational capabilities.

Table 2-2. *Risk Resilience capability map*

	Level 1 Initial	Level 2 Basic	Level 3 Standard	Level 4 Competing	Level 5 Leading
Scope or Reach	Regulatory	Corporate	Functional	Cross-functional (end-to-end)	Cross-organization (extended enterprise)
Key Attributes	Legal, Ad hoc practices	Mandatory, Requirement driven, Reactive processes	Operationally oriented, Event or risk driven	Policy-centric, Proactive planning	Value and life cycle driven, Measurement and monitoring

It is obvious in this capability map, initially business leaders and organizations in general are focused on what must be absolutely addressed and managed, that is, risk related to legal compliance. The scope of risk management increases as the business engagement model expands beyond the internal processes. In terms of organizational competencies, initially most of the risk-related practices, including discovery and mitigation, are reactive. Competent organizations become proactive with defined processes, and even more effective and risk resilient with the ability to sense things before they happen. It is not expected, and not even recommended, that every organization must seek to be level 5 in all capabilities. The emphasis must be on value generation, including being risk resilient, for the business engagement level. Use Figure 2-1 to determine the right place on the capability map based on the assessment of your engagement model.

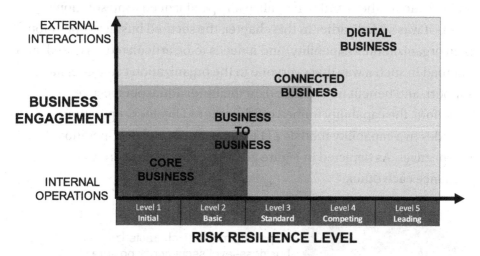

Figure 2-1. *Business Engagement vs. Resilience Level*

With the introduction of the business engagement model and risk resilience capability map, an organization can determine how secure their business operations need to be.

This is a first step in achieving and sustaining secured business operations as an organizational capability. In the next section and subsequent chapters, additional components of this framework are explained, and the remaining steps are outlined for making it happen in any organization.

Achieving and Sustaining Secured Business Operations

We understand businesses are different, and there are many different solutions to a problem, yet we also see how people leverage their experiences across functions, organizations, industries, and even cultures. The framework and approach for achieving and sustaining secured business operations is industry, language, and technology agnostic. At the same time, it allows an organization to quickly focus on what is important and relevant to them and personalize for specific needs and solutions.

As it was stated earlier in this chapter, the secured business operation is an organizational capability, and it needs to be articulated, assessed, and planned in such a way that everyone in the organization can understand, support, and benefit from it based on their individual perspective. Therefore, the capability framework for secured business operations includes two capability models – (1) Management and (2) Operational perspectives. As depicted in Figure 2-2, these two models drive and influence each other.

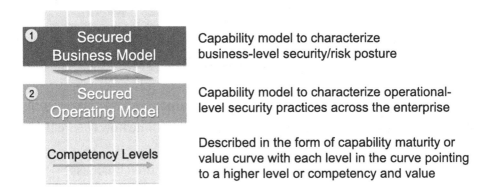

Figure 2-2. *Capability Models*

Almost all solution frameworks and methodologies emphasize alignment with business objectives, but generally lack specificity in helping people in finding the alignment. The biggest barrier in any alignment and decision making is that people can only plan based on what they know. So, how do people learn more and sooner?

It is very hard to achieve, let alone sustain, if we don't begin with the end in mind. The secured business model is the first capability model from a business perspective, breaking down the barriers to alignment and learning.

For secured business operations, what should business leaders be asking, planning, and managing? In the secured business model, five performances (5 Ps) domains are defined for business management to identify the risk posture of their business operations. Figure 2-3 outlines 5 Ps with the business intent they address.

Figure 2-3. *5 Ps of Secured Business Model*

Each of the 5 Ps has multiple capability dimensions. Each dimension is characterized across 5 maturity levels. For example, Prevent Domain includes what kind of unauthorized access and what kind of information leakage you want to prevent as a business. The maturity levels, progressively, define the types of unauthorized access or leakage you can be preventing. The higher the maturity, the broader the reach and range of prevention. Based on your business engagement model, you should be able to identify where you need to be across these 5 Ps, evaluate where you are, and what you could be doing to close the gap.

The secured business model acts as a planning and execution guide as well as an accountability and value management tool for the organization, a critical requirement of an effective alignment and oversight. See Chapter 3 for the detailed, inside view of the secured business model.

With the knowledge of "what" is needed across 5 Ps, the organization can now proceed to assess and plan the operational practices needed to support the 5 Ps. The operational practices are encapsulated in the secured operating model. See Figure 2-4 for various operational domains included in the model.

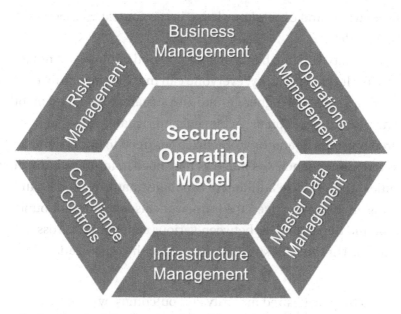

Figure 2-4. *Secured Operating Model*

The secured operating model provides a 360° view of various cross-functional, operational capabilities needed for achieving and sustaining secured business operations. The six capability domains shown in Figure 2-4 include 21 critical capabilities every organization should be regularly evaluating and improving in alignment with the secured business model. Just like 5 Ps in secured business model, 21 critical capabilities in secured operating model are also characterized along the 5 maturity levels. For example, Business Management includes change management, governance, and KPI measurement as three critical capabilities. As noted in the previous chapter, most of the existing operational and technical practices and frameworks are operational and technical in content. They form the underpinning, supporting practices for the capabilities in the secured operating model. Therefore, the secured operating model acts as a unifying capability model by accounting and incorporating current practices and solutions. The organizations can assess the current capabilities built on current industry practices and solutions, and leverage other frameworks and expert knowledge in the context of a secured operating model.

We can't clap with one hand, at least not loud enough and not for long. At a low level of maturity, everyone can make some improvements on their own. To get to a higher ground and sustain, we depend on others as much as they depend on us. Achieving and sustaining higher maturity in secured business operations, organizations need to understand and address interdependencies as much as they need to improve individual capabilities. Therefore, in addition to capability maturity models and underlying enabling practices, the framework also includes inbound and outbound dependencies between various capabilities across the organization. This body of knowledge can help the organization on two fronts –

1. Achieving desired maturity and outcomes by recognizing and addressing gaps in the dependent capabilities.

2. Driving change and communicating value by enabling upstream capabilities to improve their maturity.

See Figure 2-5 as an example of how a dependency map can help understand and manage risk and value.

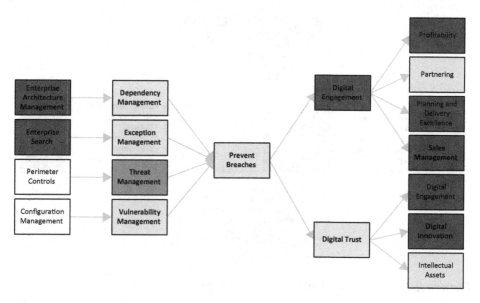

Figure 2-5. *Capability Dependency Map*

A body of knowledge is critical, but, on its own, is neither sufficient nor does it guarantee successful adoption and implementation. We have seen technologies failing to deliver expected results, and training courses failing to change behavior. To close the gap between information and transformation, there is a need of an execution discipline by leveraging the body of knowledge for desired outcomes. Therefore, in the overall framework for secured business operations, a secured management model is included. Figure 2-6 provides the high-level model that is explored in detail in Chapter 5.

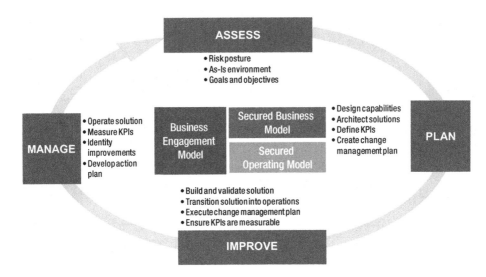

Figure 2-6. *Secured Management Model*

The secured management model is an outcome-oriented approach to sustain secured business operations in a scalable way holistically from a people, process, information, and technology perspective. It incorporates cumulative learning from many process management practices, such as lean six-sigma, value management, and program management. The model emphasizes measurement and includes a list of potential KPIs that organizations can use at each level of maturity in order to monitor progress and impact.

So far, we have introduced many components of the framework for achieving and sustaining secured business operations. The framework details follow in subsequent chapters. Let's quickly summarize how one can use the framework for managing cyber and security risks, as well as create competitive advantage with secured business operations as an organizational capability.

1. Use the business engagement model to identify the kind of interactions with employees, customers, and partners. The depth and breadth of the engagement defines the cyber risk exposure the organization needs to manage.

2. Use the secured business model to identify what an organization must secure while enabling the business engagement. The model includes a capability maturity model addressing 5 Ps of risk posture – Prevent, Protect, People, Policy, and Profile. Using the model, business leaders can clearly articulate their risk posture, provide necessary guidance, and monitor organization performance against desired outcomes.

3. Use the secured operating model to assess, develop, and maintain the required practices involving people, process, information, and technology for secured business operations, guided by the risk posture defined using a secured business model.

4. Use the secured management model to implement the discipline necessary to adjust and sustain secured business operations aligned with the business engagement model.

Figure 2-7 outlines the purpose of each model in the framework for secured business operations.

Figure 2-7. *Secured Business Operations*

Now, let's review two use cases - how the framework was used by different organizations. In the current business environment, you may find your organization somewhere in between the two studied organizations. During the initial assessment and follow-through planning in these organizations and otherwise, we noticed the following:

- Increased business involvement and accountability. Cybersecurity is no longer an IT-centric topic.

- Change in business and IT posture toward risk management. They started moving from being risk-averse toward risk-managed in their decision making and planning.

- Knowledge of "unknowns" that helped in planning. Because of unknowns, there was a lot of fear that was leading to overengineering and overspending.

- By-design mindset. Everyone begins to think about their role and responsibility in achieving and sustaining secured business operations.

Manufacturing Organization (B2B Engagement Model)

An industrial product manufacturing and distribution organization primarily works with other business organizations, rather than the end-user consumers. It has multiple manufacturing and warehouse locations. It has strategic and operationally integrated partnerships with a set of customers and suppliers.

Based on its interaction and flow of information with customers and partners, it was determined that the business engagement model was to be Business to Business (B2B). Over time, it may evolve into a connected business as it expands collaboration and integration beyond supply chain, order processing, shipping, and support. As a conservative and cautious organization, the business and IT management have been very methodical in leveraging new technologies, particularly for communicating and sharing information outside the company. In spite of careful planning and safety-first culture, the management felt pressure on both fronts – increasing security-related cost and fear, and pressure from customers and partners for more and more electronic processing and timely information. Business leadership along with the CIO decided to take an outside-in or business-centric view of their security practices, and find a happy medium between required innovation in their business processes and resistance to change due to security risk.

A small project team consisting of business, IT, and external consultants worked for about six weeks in assessing the current practices and developing the recommendations. The team leveraged the secured business capability maturity model to survey many business senior- and middle-level managers to capture their thoughts on the security posture. As expected, there was a sufficient variability in responses due to different perceptions or varying maturity across business processes. As shown in Figure 2-8, the average maturity of many of their 5P capabilities was close to level 2. Referring back to Figure 2-1, for a B2B organization seeking to become better connected with its customers and partners, being level 2 is not a bad place to be. Definitely, there were areas they needed to improve to reduce the unnecessary risk exposure.

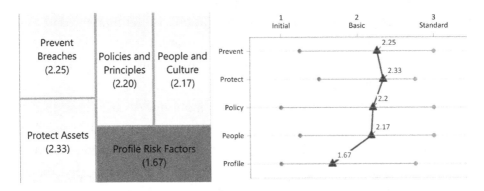

Figure 2-8. *Assessment - Secured Business Model*

Once the management understood the current risk posture, the project team proceeded to assess current practices. It invited business and IT process owners and stakeholders to participate in a survey. As processes are integrated with customers and partners, the team decided to invite select customers and partners to understand their point of view. A heat map of current capabilities based on a secured operating model was produced, highlighting the level of competency in various areas. Figure 2-9 shows that most of the operational capabilities were between maturity levels 2 and 3. Dependency management and life cycle management capabilities were operating even at lower maturity levels than 2.

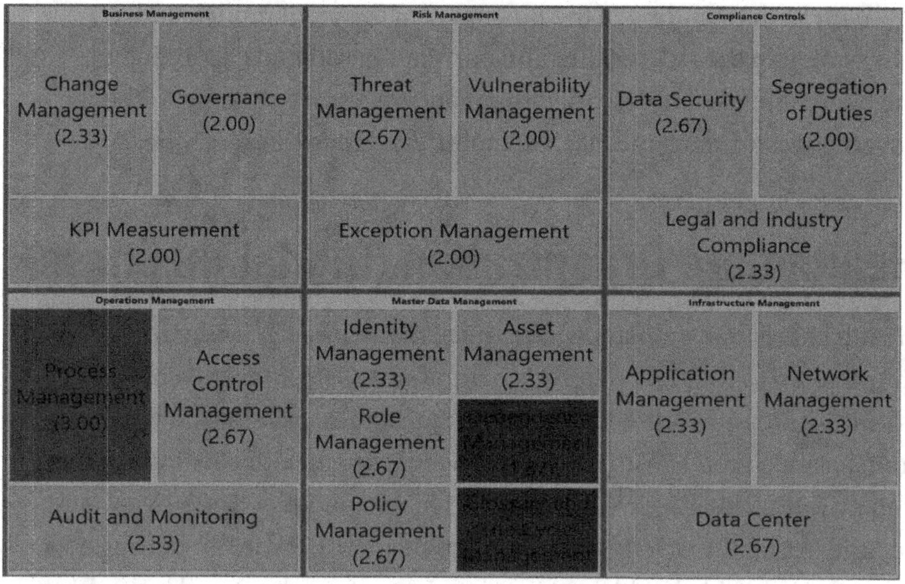

Business Management		Risk Management		Compliance Controls	
Change Management (2.33)	Governance (2.00)	Threat Management (2.67)	Vulnerability Management (2.00)	Data Security (2.67)	Segregation of Duties (2.00)
KPI Measurement (2.00)		Exception Management (2.00)		Legal and Industry Compliance (2.33)	
Operations Management		Master Data Management		Infrastructure Management	
Process Management (3.00)	Access Control Management (2.67)	Identity Management (2.33)	Asset Management (2.33)	Application Management (2.33)	Network Management (2.33)
		Role Management (2.67)			
Audit and Monitoring (2.33)		Policy Management (2.67)		Data Center (2.67)	

Figure 2-9. *Assessment - Secured Operating Model*

Although many aspects of the assessment were obvious, there were a couple of interesting observations.

1. A few current practices were overinvested based on the business engagement model and risk posture identified from the secure business model. Continued investment or improvement in these areas was contributing to the cost but not necessarily the value.

2. Some areas were overlooked or significantly underinvested, that is, below desired maturity level, negatively impacting overall posture and return on other capabilities.

With understanding of the business engagement model, and assessment of the risk posture and current operational capabilities, the board and executive leadership made necessary changes to the governance, funding, metrics, execution, and reporting activities.

Health Care Organization (Digital Business)

Health care is one industry where time is of an essence and right information to the right people is paramount. Care and convenience is putting pressure on security and risk measures. Health care is transforming greatly with the focus on digitizing health care information and providing health care services virtually to patients. The privacy and security regulations, HIPAA, PHI, PCI, PII, and EDPA are all putting a lot of controls to provide health care services in a safe manner and by keeping the consumer, patient, in mind. With advancement in technologies, medical devices and the desire to share information with various parties in real time for timely and quality care while reducing the cost of care, it is quite evident that the business engagement model for most health care organizations can be categorized as digital business.

To provide secured patient care services and securely manage patient health information, health care providers, insurance organizations, and pharmaceuticals are required to work in tight integration while abiding to all regulatory requirements. Achieving and sustaining end-to-end secured business operations is more challenging in heavily siloed and disjointed systems environment. As digitization plays the significant role, the approach was taken to look into the full spectrum of the five Ps of the secured business model as an internationally recognized health care provider. The board and the senior leadership understood the profiles of risks, associated vulnerabilities, and exceptions; and the business importance of preventing breaches and protecting assets was realized. The understanding led to improving policies by creating a supporting executive-level governance committee for making decisions and developing appropriate policies. The core team of 50 plus subject-matter experts and consultants was formed to focus on developing the strategy and operationalization of secured business operations by changing the mindset of people. To achieve the business goals of guest-friendly patient care, extending reach to global health care providers and pharmaceuticals in a trustworthy, reliable, and safe manner, a multimillion and multiyear enterprise-level strategic initiative was spawned.

Using the secured operating model, the following strategic business-critical initiatives were initiated for planning and overall enterprise architecture purposes:

Business Management – The cross-functional governance committee, including health care providing hospitals, finance, legal, and operations, was established with the focus on providing the secured health care services.

Operations Management – Multiple initiatives were in focus for securing the operations from payment cards processing, health care and supporting services management, patient identity and health information, IT operations, and network operations perspective.

Risk Management – The risk profiles were established to understand, prioritize, manage, and execute projects to eliminate associated vulnerabilities and exceptions for the overall management of the relevant risks.

Compliance Controls – To meet the regulatory requirements, enterprise-level architecture was established for aligning business and technology architecture and meeting the compliance controls requirements in a sustainable manner.

Infrastructure Management – The vulnerabilities associated with networks, data center servers, storage, and middleware posed the fundamental risks for achieving the desired level of security associated with cybercrime and securing the business operations.

Master Data Management – The data associated with managed assets, patients, health care provider workforce, other providers, research, and insurance companies were not centrally managed and had vulnerabilities posing security risks.

To start with, the board decided to give importance to strengthen the foundation elements and the focus was given to manage the associated infrastructure risks. The strategic program was spawned with well-defined key performance indicators and associated measurements to successful manage such a business-critical initiative using the execution discipline defined by the secured management model.

The administrators recognized that this is a journey and they are now engaged on a continuum basis to ensure new capabilities developed based on the risks associated with the change or advancements in interactions with people and systems in the ecosystem.

Achieving and Sustaining Secured Business Operations in Your Organization

A change and persistent transformation starts with awareness. As you can see through the above case studies, many people in these organizations were taking care of the security, doing more than necessary in some cases while being unaware of many other things. How do you know your weak links? How do you know that you are doing the right things, not just for today but for tomorrow as well? If you begin with the end in mind, every step you take will help you achieve and sustain progress.

Therefore, awareness among your board and senior management for a secured business operation is critical for creating a competitive edge for your business growth; and just like other critical capabilities, they must take active interest in building and maintaining this capability. Use the body of knowledge in this book and state of your organization for creating the required management mindset. You may conduct an initial, quick assessment using the business engagement model and 5 Ps in the secured business model to create awareness and support.

As we stated earlier, secured business operations are an organizational capability. It means you would need representation and engagement of various functions and roles across the organization. Conduct a survey using the business engagement model, secured business model, and secured operating model with a broader group of people with follow-up interviews with select people. These models and assessments will drive learning, common language, and shared objectives across the organization.

Based on the gaps between the current and desired risk posture, develop a plan for addressing the 5 Ps. Start by assessing, building, and maintaining the profile of various vulnerabilities in your business operations. Ensure that you have business-driven policies and holistic governance in place to prevent breaches and protect enterprise-level business operations internally and externally with employees, customers, partners, and suppliers. The behavior and attitude of the people define the culture of the enterprise. Generally, people are often the weakest links in sustaining secured business operations.

Strengthen your culture and ensure people who are part of your workforce, including internally and externally, are well educated on an ongoing basis regarding the security measures.

The subsequent chapters provide detailed explanation of the framework and the models introduced in this chapter. They also include underlying practices, dependencies, and metrics to help you further in developing plans and operationalizing the framework for achieving and sustaining secured business operations in your organization.

CHAPTER 3

Secured Business Model

Business and trust are two sides of the same coin. You can't have one without the other. So, let's manage them as one.

Achieving and Sustaining Secured Business Operations Starts with Business

No organization wants to take unnecessary risk. No business leader wants to do anything intentionally that would negatively harm the organization or themselves. Every business leader is accountable for something specific that eventually contributes to desired business outcomes. Business leaders set the framework and direction for the team to do the right things and believe they are doing the right things. If this is the case, we ask, why are business leaders concerned about security? Why don't business managers like the security solutions proposed by Information Technology (IT) teams? Why do organizations continue to be surprised by security incidents? The answer seems to be obvious – misplaced accountability[1]

---

[1]Peter Bregman, "The Right Way to Hold People Accountable," *Harvard Business Review*, January 11, 2016, https://hbr.org/2016/01/the-right-way-to-hold-people-accountable.

for securing business operations. Business thinks IT is accountable for security, but IT alone cannot set the clear expectations, develop the clear capability, set the key performance indicators for the business outcome, and take appropriate risks.

In the previous chapter, we introduced a top-down approach with the secured business model for remediating the issues around accountability, direction, and alignment across the organization. In this chapter, we provide the details of this model to elaborate what it is and how it can be used by the business leaders for planning, prioritizing, communicating, and monitoring the state of capabilities required for secured business operations.

The secured business model provides a bridge between the business objectives and underlying business practices and technology solutions for secured business operations. The model helps business leaders articulate their goals and objectives into a set of clear and directional statements about what must be prevented or protected, ensure alignment, establish the appropriate freedom within the framework, set expectations, and monitor progress and outcomes. This model helps operational and line managers in scoping, driving cross-functional alignment, managing a portfolio, and measuring and communicating the value of their initiatives. The next chapter provides the detailed insight into the secured operating model in support of the secured business model.

Secured Business Model and Five Ps

The heart of every effective business management is a business model, defining the purpose, value proposition, and core – differentiating capabilities. For secured business operations, the Secured Business Model provides an information security capability map from a business perspective. It is used to determine the organization's current risk posture, and the required capabilities for the required secured business posture.

In addition, the model provides the guidance for closing the gaps and acts as a vehicle for monitoring the execution. The capabilities are organized in five performance domains. Each performance domain includes a set of capability building blocks. Each capability building block is characterized across five maturity or performance levels. Figure 3-1 outlines the five Ps with their top-level capability building blocks.

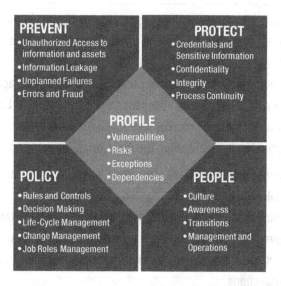

PREVENT
- Unauthorized Access to information and assets
- Information Leakage
- Unplanned Failures
- Errors and Fraud

PROTECT
- Credentials and Sensitive Information
- Confidentiality
- Integrity
- Process Continuity

PROFILE
- Vulnerabilities
- Risks
- Exceptions
- Dependencies

POLICY
- Rules and Controls
- Decision Making
- Life-Cycle Management
- Change Management
- Job Roles Management

PEOPLE
- Culture
- Awareness
- Transitions
- Management and Operations

Figure 3-1. *Secured Business Model with 5 Ps Details*

One cannot clap with one hand. Business leaders must focus on all these five performance domains collectively to ensure that they have the right capabilities and are providing a clear direction to everyone in the organization for conducting business operations with the required security risk resilience.

PREVENT performance domain represents what an organization is preventing or should be preventing from happening. Any occurrence of unauthorized access, leakage, failure, denial of service, or errors and fraud will have a detrimental impact on the organization's ability to conduct and maintain business operations.

Table 3-1 lists the key capabilities in the prevent domain. Based on the current and desired business engagement with customers, partners, and employees, business management can identify what must be prevented.

Table 3-1. *Prevent Domain*

Prevent Capability Building Blocks

Unauthorized Access	Today, most organizational assets are digitized. Limiting the right access to the right people at the right time is the most crucial to prevent cyber-attacks. Prevent unauthorized access and identify undesired access granted. The extent of prevention depends upon the extent of business engagement and process/system exposure. Business must take ownership in establishing the appropriate access controls.
Information Leakage	Prevent unintended and unplanned leakage of information and intellectual property (IP) of the organization. Business must define the type of information and IP that must be prevented from any leakage, for example, information related to employees, customers, partners, products, services, and associated transactions.
Unplanned Failures	Unplanned disruption in the functioning of a core organization and information assets could pose risk to business continuity and security of business operations. Prevent unplanned and unnecessary failures in ongoing operations for mitigating associated business continuity risks. Business must make sure all aspects of secured business operations are considered holistically for preventing unplanned failures.
Errors and Fraud	Prevent human errors and potential fraud by internal or external people or organizations. Technology cannot prevent all errors. Business has the knowledge of processes and the context. Business must define what errors and fraud must be prevented.

The PROTECT performance domain represents what is or must be guarded from any lasting damage to integrity and trust within and outside the organization.

Table 3-2 lists the key capabilities in the protect domain. Not all information requires the same kind or level of protection. Business must define what information is critical to the organization and then plan and manage its protection from any undue harm.

Table 3-2. *Protect Domain*

Protect Capability Building Blocks	
Credentials and Sensitive Information	Protect and preserve credentials and any information deemed sensitive by the organization from any harm. Business must take ownership in defining the credentials and sensitive information and appropriate controls for guarding such information.
Integrity	Protect information from any tempering during transmission of the information, or while being kept in any kind of storage. It is required for the information to be trusted by the recipient or consumer. Business must define appropriate rules to maintain the integrity of information produced or acquired.
Confidentiality	Protect privacy of information and transaction while communicating or sharing information between people, processes, and devices regardless of their location or means of communication. Business only can define the privacy level required and must create the capability to define these levels and associate an appropriate level to every information asset.

(*continued*)

Table 3-2. (*continued*)

Protect Capability Building Blocks

Process Continuity	Protect people, processes, interactions, and transactions from disruptions of any kind, for example, denial of service, could pose risk and lead into security breaches. The continuity in business terms is about a smooth and uninterrupted flow of information. Business must identify what must be protected for business continuity and ensure the appropriate measures are in place.

POLICY performance domain addresses the polity or governance with appropriate organizational policies, decision rights, and processes for safe and secure business operations.

Table 3-3 lists the key capabilities in the policy domain.

Table 3-3. *POLICY Domain*

Policy Capability Building Blocks

Rules and Controls	A control is an actionable pre-decided policy statement for offering secured business operations for a business situation or for an external regulatory requirement. This control requires one or more rules to put it into action. A rule is a binding statement that is set for managing some business situation. A rule can be leveraged by one or more controls. Establish guiding principles, governing rules, and controls for ensuring appropriate design and implementation of security-related procedures. It is important that business takes accountability to define these rules and controls for securing business operations.

(*continued*)

Table 3-3. (*continued*)

Policy Capability Building Blocks

Decision Making	A decision for planning and managing security risk may require support of business leaders across business functions. Business must define decisions rights, processes, and measures for ensuring appropriate behavior across the organization in a structured manner.
Life Cycle Management	Every asset has a useful life beyond which its value deteriorates. To sustain secured business operations through business innovations or changes in the business environment, business management must review, replace, and retire past decisions, controls, rules, processes, and structures to keep them aligned with the changing business dynamics. Business must take responsibility to define life cycle management of rules and controls for managing, at all times, desired security risk levels.
Change Management	Business leaders are periodically making strategic and tactical decisions, requiring either changes in the existing capabilities, or, development of new capabilities. Introduction of a new or enhanced capability can impact the security aspect of the business operations, or it may be required to ensure new business operations are optimal and secured. To ensure value is created, security risks are mitigated, operations remain secured, and the business management must take the ownership and accountability seriously to see that the change happens as expected in the organization.
Job Roles	People are an integral part of every business process. In additional to functional skills for the job, people need to have appropriate security-related skills for secured business operations. It is not sufficient for Human Resources to define and manage job roles. Business managers know their business processes and understand potential exposure. They must consider the security aspect of the process in defining roles and organizing skills.

41

The PEOPLE performance domain represents the people-centric management responsibilities and activities for ensuring ongoing secured business operations. Every business activity and outcome requires a combination of people, process, information, and technology. As much as the human element could add intelligence, flexibility, and compassion to any business process, it also introduces a security risk. The people domain defines intangible and tangible management actions for appropriate culture, workforce transitions, and awareness and readiness for managing the security risk.

Table 3-4 lists the key capabilities in the people domain.

Table 3-4. *PEOPLE Domain*

People Capability Building Blocks	
Culture	Beliefs, behavior, attitude, and adoption of security mindset and risk posture of people in the organization. Culture defines what people in the organization will do when they encounter a situation.
	Unless machines are making all the decisions, it is important that leadership is promoting and driving the appropriate culture for secured business operations under all circumstances.
Awareness	Most of the security incidents in an organization happen due to lack of awareness and readiness. In many cases, people represent the first or the last mile in business interactions. People can only make decisions and take actions based on what they know.
	Individual responsibility starts with business leaders making sure that people are aware of the security implications and are prepared to take appropriate actions.

(continued)

Table 3-4. (*continued*)

People Capability Building Blocks

Transitions	It is given that people will change their roles and new people will take over the tasks. The transition should not only address the access controls but also the individual knowledge related to security in the context of the tasks being transitioned. Business must define the type and extent of access controls and security knowledge needed for a job, and ensure that access and knowledge transfer is managed across transitions.
Management and Operations	Having capability for setting the direction, driving change and accountability, ensuring integration across strategic and execution processes, managing development, and adoption of security practices across the organization. Just like business management is anticipating, planning and driving innovative business capabilities, business should be evaluating and planning security capabilities, policies, and practices for sustaining secured business operations through the change in business.

The PROFILE performance domain defines what the organization must know to plan and maintain secured business operations. It includes knowledge of vulnerabilities, exceptions, risks, and dependencies in the organizations across people, process, information, and technologies. Without this knowledge, organizations may not be as proactive in anticipating and addressing potential incidents. In many ways, this domain supports all other performance domains.

Table 3-5 lists the key capabilities in the profile domain.

Table 3-5. *PROFILE Domain*

Profile Capability Building Blocks

Vulnerabilities	A vulnerability is a weakness that can be exploited in reducing an organization's risk resilience. A vulnerability can be anywhere across people, business process, and technologies. Organization must profile current and potential internal and external vulnerabilities.
Risks	Security risks have potential to impact an organization brand along with potential to impact the profitability and/or revenue growth. Managing such risks is critical for sustaining secured business operations. Business leaders must take responsibility for profiling of security risks and mitigation plans from a business perspective.
Exceptions	Security exceptions need to be monitored and managed. Over time, an exception may become a vulnerability or a risk. Business must ensure they have capability to identify exceptions and manage exceptions over time to achieve desired risk resilience.
Dependencies	Every business outcome requires cross-functional, in many cases cross-organizational, collaboration. The management needs to understand interdependencies to effectively manage the security risk in any business operation. Organization must profile internal and external dependencies across people, process, technologies, and information assets.

Secured Business Model Capability Maturity Levels as a Value Road Map

Every organization, regardless of the industry, must ensure that the security risk resilience is in alignment with the business engagement model and organization's goals. In the previous chapter (see Figures 2-1 and 2-3), we explained the business engagement model, how an organization can determine the engagement type and corresponding security risk resilience level. Each risk resilience level requires a set of organizational capabilities and practices. So, the obvious question is what are those capabilities for a risk resilience level? In the previous section, we identified five performance domains (5 Ps) of the secured business model. Each of these performance domains can be further described in the form of a capability maturity model, where a maturity level can be viewed as capability requirements to achieve a level of risk resilience.

Figure 3-2 summarizes the capability maturity model for each of the 5 Ps in the secured business model. The detailed, up-to-date maturity model of all capabilities in the 5 Ps can be accessed from securedbusinessops.com.

Capability Domains	Level 1 Initial	Level 2 Basic	Level 3 Standard	Level 4 Competing	Level 5 Leading
Prevent	Prevent unauthorized access of core assets for regulatory compliance	Prevent leakage of information mandated by corporate policies	Prevent unnecessary failures in time-sensitive processes	Proactively prevent errors and frauds in all managed assets in the enterprise	Prevent interruptions, errors and leakage across the ecosystem
Protect	Protect credentials and sensitive info per legal and regulations	Protect core managed assets privacy and confidentiality	Protect data accuracy and integrity of business important managed assets	Protect and manage info and transactions shared with external entities	Proactively protect and manage across channels & the operations lifecycle
People	People awareness and compliance training	Readiness training and monitoring for corporate policies	Manage transitions and people readiness for planning and operations	Risk-based decisioning skills. Extend readiness to core partners	Proactive preparedness of customers and partners addressing all channels
Policy	Defined legal and regulatory policies and management authority.	Defined job roles and governing structure.	Info classification and Life cycle policies. Proactively mitigate known risks	Cross-functional and change management policies. Policy-driven processes	Accounts for interactions with external entities. Value-driven behavior
Profile	Adhoc risk profiles for core managed assets	Profile risk and associated registers to manage risks and support assessments	Profile dependencies and exceptions to proactively manage known risks	Monitor and profile potential vulnerabilities and external dependencies	Define and profile impact and performance metrics with risks across the ecosystem and channels

Figure 3-2. *Secured Business Model Summary Capability Map*

Each maturity level identifies what capabilities an organization must have across the 5 Ps. This model is not about how an organization will accomplish these capabilities. We will be discussing that in the next chapter.

The capability maturity model is a progressive and cumulative model, that is, capabilities at one level builds upon the capabilities at previous levels. It also means that an organization must have capabilities from previous levels to be considered for the next level of maturity. For example, at a lower level of maturity, an organization may only consider preventing unauthorized access to a physical location or systems storing critical business information. As the organization expands interaction with customers and partners, the organization must prevent unauthorized access to business transactions and documents, achieving the next level of maturity. Depending upon the nature of collaboration and use of digital assets, organizations may need to enhance its capabilities in preventing unauthorized access to distributed content, further driving the level of maturity and risk resilience.

Because of the progressive nature of the capability maturity model, it can easily be used as a value or capability improvement road map. As described in Figure 2-3 in the previous chapter, an organization that is already a connected business or seeking to be one, the target risk resilience level should be at least level 4 – Competing. It means, business management should be prioritizing and planning capabilities, and monitoring progress toward level 4. The capability gap between the current and desired state defines the improvement road map.

It is expected that an organization may not be at a particular level across all 5 Ps. It is possible that an organization might have focused on a few select capabilities or overinvested in some capabilities to address specific situations or in response to market news. Just like it is hard to stay comfortable and stable while sitting on a stool with legs of varied sizes, organizations can't ensure and sustain secured business operations if the organization does not make progress toward the required maturity level across all 5 Ps.

In a large organization with multiple business segments or organizational units, it is quite possible that various segments may be at different maturity levels. It is not important that all of them be at the same level of maturity, but it is critical that each segment is at the right level for the required risk resilience in business activities performed by the people, processes, and systems in that segment. Using the secured business model, each segment can evaluate its current state and identify the desired state, and use the gap for developing the improvement road map.

Secured Business Model Is a Bridge Between Business Engagement and Operating Model

In Chapter 2, Figure 2-9 described the connected layers of the Secured Business Operations. The Secured Business Model is the critical layer between business engagement and the secured operating model. Business leaders and managers own the responsibility and accountability in defining the state of business engagement and required capabilities across 5 Ps in the secured business model. The following Figure 3-3 shows the correlation between various business engagement models and 5 Ps of secured business model.

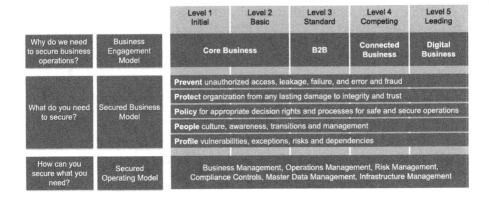

Figure 3-3. *Secured Business Model – A Bridge*

Once the required capabilities in the secured business model are defined, the organization is ready to evaluate and plan capabilities in the secured operating model. The next chapter provides details of the secured operating model.

CHAPTER 4

Secured Operating Model

The operating rhythm without the predictable behavior in sensing and responding to the events that we didn't anticipate is a fire drill.

Realizing Secured Business Operations

The objectives, the requirements, the plans – help us create a desire for change and define a direction, but they are not sufficient to ensure we get to our intended destination. In Chapter 2, we discussed the business engagement model for defining the level of risk resilience required to support secured business interactions with customers, partners, and employees inside and outside the organizational boundary. In Chapter 3, we discussed the secured business model with five performance domains (5Ps), providing a set of capabilities and their desired levels of maturity for a given risk resilience posture. Both the business engagement and secured business models are designed to guide business management in defining and justifying the outcomes, that is, what and why the organization must achieve for safe and secure business operations.

© Neelesh Ajmani and Dinesh Kumar 2017
N. Ajmani and D. Kumar, *Achieving and Sustaining Secured Business Operations*,
https://doi.org/10.1007/978-1-4842-3099-2_4

In this chapter, we focus on how organizations can achieve and sustain secured business operations. The secured operating model provides an actionable body of knowledge in understanding, identifying, and implementing necessary operational capabilities for realizing the desired outcomes defined in the secured business model. Why the secured operating model when we have many operational frameworks such as NIST 800-171, NIST 800-53, ISO 27001/27002, and many others? There is no doubt these frameworks provide a depth of knowledge that no single person or organization can develop and organize. These frameworks focus on security policies, procedures, and controls, providing a highly prescriptive content for auditors, implementers, and practitioners. It is left up to the organization to figure out the extent of relevancy and develop a road map for implementing policies, procedures, and controls. Organizations tend to underplan or overengineer the implementation due to lack of structured understanding, alignment, prioritization, and business case for policies, procedures, and controls in the context of organizational and business capabilities. Just like when digging a hole, it is difficult to be wide and deep at the same time, most of these technical frameworks provide an excellent depth in cybersecurity and risk management but tend to ignore other capabilities needed to drive overall organizational maturity and effectiveness even in their area of focus. The secured operating model provides the bridge between what the organization wants to secure in the form of a secured business model and the specific best practices and implementation described in these frameworks. Figure 4-1 articulates the dependencies and relationship between various layers of the body of knowledge in achieving and sustaining secured business operations.

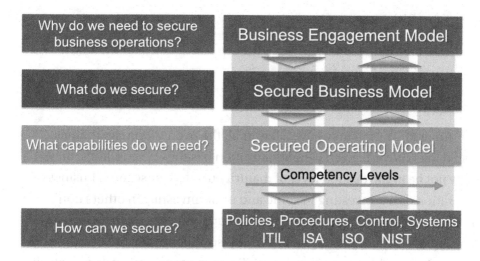

Figure 4-1. Secured Operating Model and Industry Frameworks

The secured operating model includes a set of core capabilities along with their maturity levels. The model also includes underlying practices derived from various best practices and security frameworks. The model allows organizations to focus on the capabilities. It is the capabilities that enable organizations to sense, respond, and operate in a predicable manner even in previously unknown situations. Every time there is a security breach, it doesn't do any good if the organization scrambles and comes up with an excuse of not seeing it before. With the secured operating model, the organizations can build and maintain the required capabilities to achieve and sustain secured business operations.

Components of Secured Operating Model

The secured operating model consists of twenty-one operational capabilities organized into the following six capability domains.

1. Business Management

2. Operations Management

3. Risk Management

4. Compliance Controls

5. Master Data Management

6. Infrastructure Management

An organization may have a few or all the twenty-one capabilities listed in Figure 4-3. Even if an organization has these capabilities, they may not be at the desired level of maturity needed for secured business operations. Overinvesting in some and underinvesting in others don't make organizations safe and secure. All capabilities need to be focused and sufficiently advanced to achieve and sustain the desired outcomes. Figure 4-2 provides a top-level capability map at various levels of maturity. This map can be used to understand where we are and where we need to be in operating practices, aligned with the required capabilities in the 5 Ps defined in the secured business model.[1]

Capability Domains	Level 1 Initial	Level 2 Basic	Level 3 Standard	Level 4 Competing	Level 5 Leading
Business Management	Minimal efforts on change management to achieve regulatory compliance	Corporate-level governance to prevent, protect, and manage know risks in core managed assets	Functional governance and change mgmt to manage risks for core and business important assets and processes	Enterprise governance and change management	KPIs, measurement and reporting
Operations Management	Minimal processes to manage core managed assets to achieve regulatory compliance	Defined processes for managing operations of core and business important assets	Overall on-going monitoring and operations management of all managed assets	Streamline operational policies and process for access control mgmt., audit and monitoring	KPIs to measure operations performance and effectiveness
Risk Management	React to manage risks associated with the regulatory compliance	Proactively manage risks associated with core managed assets	Proactive monitoring of risks for all managed assets. Risk factors in business cases	Risk analysis and oversight across asset lifecycle. Risk flow analysis and reporting	KPIs to measure and report effectiveness and efficiency in managing risks
Compliance Controls	Minimal regulatory compliance	Defined controls for core managed assets	Monitor and manage compliance controls for all managed assets	Controls addressing cross-functional and partner communications	Measure and report performance of compliance controls
Master Data Management	Minimal data management to achieve regulatory compliance	Defined standards for core managed assets	Enterprise practices and services for access and data management for all managed assets	Classification, life cycle and access rights for people, process, information and systems	Scope includes extended network of customers and partners
Infrastructure Management	Minimal Infrastructure for core business functions	Defined standards for managing core business functions infrastructure	Expanded infrastructure for meeting enterprise needs with cross-functional enterprise controls	Lifecycle management with appropriate security and access control management	Relevant KPIs, measurements, and reporting practices

Figure 4-2. *Secured Operating Model Summary Capability Map*

---

[1]See Chapter 3 for the Secured Business Model.

Although described as a capability maturity model, the capability map in Figure 4-2 is in fact a road map for planning operational practices. At any time, an organization may be at different maturity levels across the six capability domains. Over time, an organization cannot be too far out of step with maturity in each domain. For example, organization can't be very high in risk management and remain very basic in master data management. Sustaining secured business operations is not just about preventing something from happening; it is also about responding and recovering when something does happen. Organizations need different capabilities for proactive prevention and predictive responses to the situations. Moreover, improvement in one capability may enable another capability or reduce the demand on another capability. For example, improvement in master data management may help the organization with improved change management and governance while reducing the time and efforts required for implementing and monitoring compliance controls. Therefore, it is critical for the organizations to evaluate, understand, and plan all twenty-one capabilities under these six capability domains for appropriate maturity in core operational practices.

Figure 4-3 outlines the critical operational capabilities in each of the six capability domains.

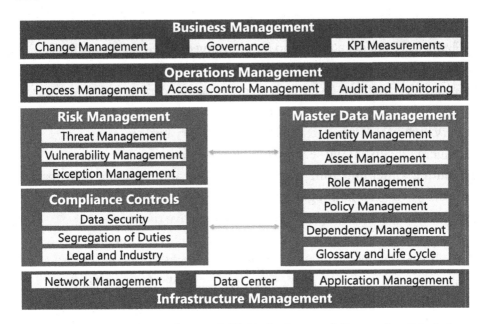

Figure 4-3. *Operational Capabilities in Secured Operating Model*

The following pages provide a summary of twenty-one capability building blocks across six capability domains.

Business Management

Business management represents a set of capabilities for the organization to plan, manage, and measure effectiveness of operational practices required for secured business operations. It is a business prerogative and issue to decide the extent the organization needs to be secured and ensure it is secured. The organizations must have relevant business management capabilities and practices. Business management, in general, may include many practices. For planning and managing the portfolio of people, process, information, and technology for secured business operations, the following three operational capabilities are the most critical to develop and mature.

1. Change Management

2. Governance

3. KPI Measurements

These capabilities are not new or unique for business management. Many times, these practices do not sufficiently consider or incorporate security-related requirements and practices or account for the impact of security. These practices are leveraged to develop a desired maturity required for achieving secured business operations. Table 4-1 provides a brief description of the three capabilities.

Table 4-1. *Business Management*

Business Management Capability Building Blocks	
Change Management	Provide relevant awareness and training to all the workforce about the capabilities/services, keeping them informed and prepared in identifying and addressing new vulnerabilities that require human behavior in addition to systematic controls.
Governance	Establish a collaborative business and IT governance structure, associated processes, and committee to govern development, maintenance, and transitioning incremental/new capabilities to conduct business operations in a secured manner.
KPI Measurements	Define, measure, and monitor key performance indicators and metrics for security effectiveness and desired outcomes.

The next section includes key practices for improving change management, governance, and KPI measurement in the organization.

Operations Management

Managing day-to-day operations is one of the core business activities in any organization. In the context of secured business operations, ongoing operational practices need to include activities related to maintaining secured operations. Therefore, Operations Management capability domain includes and primarily focuses on the following:

1. Process Management

2. Access Control Management

3. Audit and Monitoring

These operational capabilities are not new to the organization, which is good news. We just need to make sure these capabilities are enhanced so that business process design and execution are security aware and incorporates additional practices and measures for ensuring end-to-end secured business processes. Table 4-2 provides a brief description of these capabilities in a security context.

Table 4-2. Operations Management

Operations Management Capability Building Blocks

Process Management	A process is a set of interrelated activities that interact to achieve a result, for example, secured supply change management, secured channel partner communication and management, secured banking, and secured collaboration. A governance committee is responsible for ensuring appropriate processes are created, automated, and managed to meet the required and relevant security objectives.
Access Control Management	To ensure business operations are being conducted in a secured manner, it is necessary that all the managed resources have appropriate access all the time. This capability ensures that the appropriate access is granted and managed all the time.
Audit and Monitoring	This capability is required to find out at any time who is accessing what managed resources, and if there are any malicious activates going on in the enterprise environment. Based on this knowledge, appropriate risks can be created in the risk register to manage such risks appropriately.

These operational capabilities are quite interdependent and support each other. For organizational efficiency and effectiveness, all these capabilities should be advanced with appropriate design and automation. Figure 4-4 represents the relationship among these operational practices.

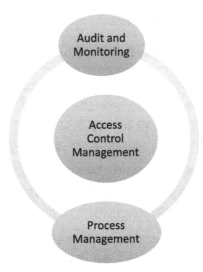

Figure 4-4. *Operations Management Operational Practices*

The access control management is supported by process management and audit and monitoring.

Risk Management

There are known security risks to the business operations due to the known vulnerabilities and their threat level. The risk management must include proper criteria for the assessment, prioritization, and treatment of risks. In the previous chapter, we discussed the security profile as one of the 5 Ps, covering vulnerabilities, dependencies, exceptions, and risks. Any vulnerability or threat is a business risk, even if it is manifested in one of the IT systems or processes. In the secured operating model, risk management is about understanding, anticipating, and managing both business and IT risks. Ultimately, business leaders are accountable and must decide the acceptable level of risk. Risk management capability includes the following:

1. Threat Management

2. Vulnerability Management

3. Exception Management

The threats, vulnerabilities, and exceptions are different, closely related terms. They are associated for managing assets. Figure 4-5 represents the relationship among managed asset, risk, threat, and vulnerability.

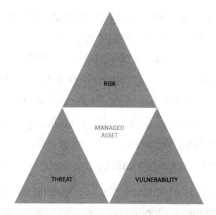

Figure 4-5. *Relationships Among Managed Asset, Risk, Threat, and Vulnerability*

Managed Asset: Anything that generates value for the business is a managed asset. It could be people, physical items, and information. People are workforce users, including employees, customers, and partners. Physical items could be office properties, products, and services with tangible or intangible value. Information could be business data, software code, and other intangible items. Businesses try to protect a managed asset.

Threat: Anything that can exploit a weakness to damage or destroy a managed asset and against which a protection is required.

Vulnerability: A weakness that can be exploited by threats to gain unauthorized access to a managed asset.

Risk: A tangible or intangible damage potentially caused due to a threat in your environment that exploits a vulnerability.

With these definitions, Table 4-3 defines each of the operating capabilities in the Risk Management domain.

Table 4-3. *Risk Management*

Risk Management Capability Building Blocks

Threat Management	Monitor and manage internal and external threats to business processes, information, systems, and assets anywhere.
Vulnerability Management	There can be many types of vulnerabilities that can pose various levels of threats to manage operations in a secured manner. These vulnerabilities could be in the Data area, Business Applications, Segregation of Duties, Lack of Policies and/or Rules, Network, Compute, Storage, Data Center, and in meeting ISO 27002, SOX, COBIT, PCI, and other types of compliance. Vulnerability Management helps in evaluating the level of threat and in mitigating threats by managing such vulnerabilities.
Exception Management	To manage exceptions that are covered by vulnerability management. Depending upon the type of exception, a special one-off solution may need to be devised, and that is why the focus should be on avoiding exceptions as much as possible.

Compliance Controls

Due to an interdependent ecosystem, and mobile and digital business information, every organization small or big needs to address confidentiality, privacy, and integrity of information. Many government and non-government entities have defined the range of controls for organizations to consider for conforming to compliance requirements or to address procedural or system risks. We have looked at hundreds of controls across various frameworks. In the secured operating model, we addressed the subject of compliance as a set of organizational and operational capabilities, supported by many of the security controls defined in industry frameworks. Table 4-4 lists these capabilities with their brief descriptions.

Table 4-4. *Compliance Controls*

Compliance Controls Capability Building Blocks	
Data Security	Data security means protecting data, such as a database, from destructive forces and from the unwanted actions of unauthorized users.
Segregation of Duties	It is the concept of having more than one person required to complete a task. In business, the separation by sharing of more than one individual in one single task is an internal control intended to prevent fraud and error.
Legal and Industry Compliance	Ensure conformance to generally accepted compliance requirements.

Compliance Controls as a capability provides the necessary business context, and a mechanism to prioritize and road map required controls for implementation and ongoing monitoring.

Master Data Management

Master data management is not a new topic. This is important for the secured operating model for two reasons.

1. The information security data domains such as Identity, Asset, Role, Policy, Dependency, and Glossary are not often considered as "master" data domains, even though they have organization-wide implications.

2. The data associated with these data domains are equally critical for business operations as other business data domains, such as Customer, Product, Supplier, and Partner. The management of security and business data is critical for executing business transactions predictably, safely, and securely.

Before discussing the master data management capabilities, we must understand the master data management principles. The principles are Data Definition, Data Integrity, Data Security, Data Services, and Data Architecture. These principles are important and required for managing data domains, identities, assets, roles, policies, dependency, and data glossary.

Data Definition

It includes defining a data domain, its ownership, identifying associated data elements, and defining each associated data element. On the business side, the definition covers the meaning, ownership, and purpose. On the technical side, it covers the data design and its implementation details. It is important to take a business perspective, as data is owned by the business and business is accountable for defining it. The meaning of a data domain clarifies the business intent, ownership defines who in the business owns it, and its purpose clarifies its business usage. The associated data elements are identified in support of business intent and usage. The meaning of each associated data element must ensure its alignment with the business intent of its data domain. Each associated data element must have a unique business purpose. The purpose of each associated data element supports the business usage of its data domain. The illustrative examples are provided in the subsequent pages in the definition and the purpose of master data management capabilities.

Data Integrity

The best way to understand this master data management principle is to first review and understand the dictionary meaning of Integrity. The origin of word integrity is from the Latin word integer, which means whole or complete. In mathematics, an integer is a whole number that has no fractions. The key characteristics of a dictionary meaning of the word integrity includes being honest and consistent with strong moral principles. Extending this definition into the dictionary definition of data integrity means the data is an exact copy of some original version, and it is absent from any unintended changes or errors in its static state or when it is transmitted or copied. In business terms, data integrity can be interpreted as the information represented by the data is validated, does not leave any ambiguity, and is authentic.

Data Security

Data security was covered under compliance controls from the regulatory requirements perspective. This master data management principle enables building foundations for achieving data security controls above and beyond compliance controls in business transactions. Business transactions rely upon master data, such as customer, product, identity, roles, and others. A typical business operation spans multiple business transactions. For secured business operations, it is imperative that data in a business transaction is secured. This is where data security principles go beyond achieving compliance controls. The data security principles include data uniqueness, data integrity, data access controls, data encryption, data decryption, and data storage. The business context, such as Sales Order, Accounts Payable, Customer Relationship Management, Market Intelligence, and others defines the usage and the characteristics of data security principles. The business context also helps in defining the requirements and cost considerations for data encryption and decryption.

Data Services

Master data is foundational for all business transactions data. For maintaining data integrity and data security, it is critical that access and maintenance of master data do not become bottlenecks. Data services, strategically defined, alleviate this situation. Direct access of master data impacts performance for processing business transactions. That is why data services principles take the center place in master data management.

Data Architecture

In the information age, data is like a bloodstream for running the business. The human body is healthy and alive when uncontaminated blood is flowing smoothly through all its veins and arteries in the entire body. The human body has a two-circuit circulatory system. One is pulmonary (for the lungs) circulation and another one is systemic (for the rest of the body) circulation. The blood is oxygenated through the lungs and this oxygenated blood flows using the framework of veins and arteries through the rest of the body. Using this analogy, entire business data is managed between master data and enterprise data. Master data management conceptually establishes data integrity and security that is extended and further maintained through enterprise data management. Data architecture is the framework that is required for managing the master data and circulating securely the enterprise data for secured business operations. The framework for master data management consists of data design incorporating data definitions, data capabilities for maintaining data integrity, data security, and data services for enabling business operations data flows.

Table 4-5 lists the master data management capabilities.

Table 4-5. *Master Data Management*

Master Data Management Capability Building Blocks

Identity Management	Identities include digital representation of the entire workforce and other managed resources associated with the business. The workforce includes, employees, contractors, and partner and customer resources who are involved in the business. The digital representation includes the storing and management of the associated identities and attributes. This capability ensures that digital representation of the identities is securely protected and poses no risks in leaking the associated details.
Asset Management	Manage physical and nonphysical assets owned by the organization.
Role Management	For secured business operations, appropriate access is required for every consumer, and that is managed automatically by assigning appropriate roles to the consumer. The consumer may be a workforce resource, a process, a system or a device. The role management capability is required to assign an appropriate role to a consumer at the start of the relationship and then update the role to account for transitions and changes in relationships.
Policy Management	To develop, deploy, and maintain life cycle of policies, with the help of a governance committee, to conduct business operations in a secured manner.
Dependency Management	Secure end-to-end business operations by ensuring all the cross-functional and organization dependencies are understood, well documented, and they all follow the same governance policies/rules to achieve the goal of secured business operations.
Glossary and Life Cycle	Define all relevant terms so that their purpose and meaning are consistently understood and used across the business organizations and the ecosystem.

The above capabilities are further explored with enabling practices in the next section.

Infrastructure Management

Securing business operations depends upon the infrastructure used for performing business activities. The security of infrastructure is the key focus area by every organization. As infrastructure is typically maintained by IT, this area does not generally get business management attention unless there is an incident impacting the business. To secure the infrastructure, many practices are considered and deployed, such as single or multi-factor authentication, single sign-on, firewalls, secured local area, wide area and wireless networks, and applications security. The Open Systems Interconnection (OSI), Figure 4-6 model is an effective way to understand, at the conceptual level, the Infrastructure elements and their security needs.

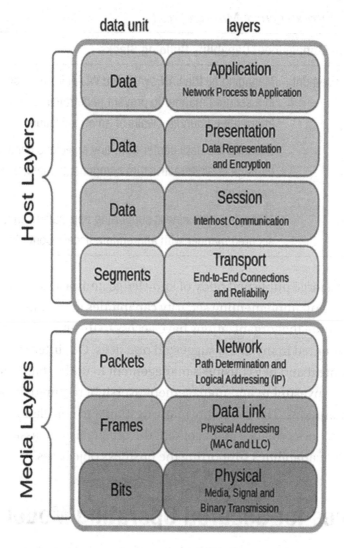

Figure 4-6. Open Systems Interconnection Model[2]

To better manage infrastructure security, we have organized infrastructure capabilities in three building blocks. Table 4-6 lists these capabilities with their brief descriptions.

---

[2]https://www.lifewire.com/open-systems-interconnection-model-816290

Table 4-6. *Infrastructure Management*

Infrastructure Management Capability Building Blocks	
Network Management	Managing all the LAN, WAN, and WLAN infrastructure in a secured manner to prevent penetration into the Information boundary walls of an organization.
Data Center Management	Securing the data center from any malicious penetration or damage of all Infrastructure components maintained in the data center.
Application Management	Managing all business supporting applications in a secured manner with appropriate access controls.

There is a large published body of knowledge and vast cybersecurity industry focus on implementing security capabilities at the Infrastructure level. We assume that organizations have access to the information and have implemented many of the suggested practices. Our intent is to add business context and help business management to understand the need and extent of investment and management oversight required for secured business operations. The capability maturity map and correlation with enabling practices provides management the mechanism to assess and plan the right capabilities supporting the business objectives.

Practices for Secured Operating Model

In the previous section, we described the twenty-one operational capabilities organized into six capability domains. In this section, we explore specific and critical implementation practices supporting these capabilities.

Business Management: Change Management

Businesses are periodically making strategic and tactical decisions for innovating, improving profitability, improving top-line growth, improving bottom-line growth, improving brand value, expanding into new markets, meeting compliance requirements, and on and on. Any such decision requires either changing the existing capabilities or developing new capabilities. A new project is spawned to develop a new or enhanced capability. In today's cybercrime environment, every project must have a security track so that the capabilities and developed solutions are secured. Most organizations follow internationally recognized standard practices for project management. Yes, over 18% of the projects fail. What does it mean? A failed project didn't deliver on expectations, either a capability was not developed or delivered, or it was not successfully transitioned into operations. In many cases, the security implications and requirements were not considered early enough in the development and transition processes. Change management is an operational practice to ensure all factors, including security, are considered and managed for a successful delivery.

Without change management, it is not possible to determine requirements from an operational perspective for a new capability or enhancement to an existing capability. Without change management, it is not possible to gauge impact on existing operations or to understand the readiness and training requirements for business users. In addition, without change management, it is not possible to determine new vulnerabilities affecting the desired security posture.

Change management is a critical operational practice for business management. Writing about change management is not a focus of this book. *Our Iceberg Is Melting: Changing and Succeeding Under Any Conditions,* by John Kotter and Holger Rathgeber, is one of the recommended books for learning about change management. In the secured business model, we talked about change management policies under the policy domain of the model. Change management as an operational capability and practice is required for supporting change management policies and secured business operations.

Business Management: Governance

Organizations generally have established corporate governance and IT governance practices for overall business management. Until recently, security was not the focus area of corporate governance. IT governance is primarily focused on technology standards and selection. The technology selection is typically based on industry ratings and reviews, and not based on the best fit for meeting the business requirements. This is generally the case with security solutions as security needs are not defined by business, and they are a risk-averse posture for the Chief Information Security Officer or IT management. The result is a continuous increase in spending on IT security while the business continues to incur financial damages from security incidents. Global spending is expected to be $101B in 2018 and $170B by 2020. As per world economy forum, businesses have security-related damages in the range of $400B–$500B with much more damage not being reported.

The accountability needs to be shared among business and IT management and the Chief Information Security Officer, mainly for defining the security requirements and supporting policies, rules, and controls. The responsibility for appropriate solution deployment and tools selection may remain with the Chief Information Security Officer, but the overall strategy and governance must be directed by the business leadership. The end-to-end secured business operations require cross-functional decision making and collaboration. An appropriate governance practice involving cross-functional business and IT executives, managers and subject-matter experts is required for ensuring timely decision making and sponsoring initiatives for achieving and sustaining secured business operations. Figure 4-7 provides an example of a governance committee structure for establishing an operational practice of governing security matters.

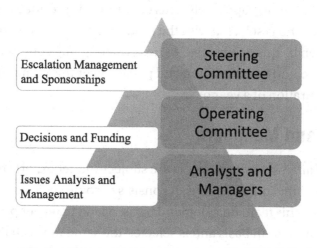

Figure 4-7. *Governance Committee Structure*

The above governance committee structure has three layers.

Steering Committee

The steering committee provides the leadership for security and other business portfolios. They manage any escalations from the operating committee. This committee sponsors security initiatives. This committee is generally presided by the Chief Operating Officer or an equivalent role.

Operating Committee

This operating committee is exclusively for security. This is formed with the help of middle-management leaders from all functional organizations. This team needs to be empowered to make security-related decisions based on the guidelines provided by the steering committee. This team should have authority to fund various related initiatives in the form of projects. For some reason, due to a complex situation and/or due to costs involved, if this team is not able to make a decision, such an issue needs to be escalated to the steering committee for the decision making and for getting funding approvals. This committee is presided over by a chairperson who is selected with the motion issued by this team and the votes taken by this committee. As this is an ongoing committee, a chairperson should be on rotation and preside over this committee for a predefined duration of a year or so.

Analysts and Managers

This team of analysts and managers are subject-matter experts from different functional organizations. It consists of some static members and some who join this team on a demand basis. A lead manager presides over this team on a rotation basis and is selected the same way a chairperson is selected for the operating committee. Any issue (vulnerability, risk, dependency, or exception) that needs action due to lack of established rules and controls is assigned to this team. Based on the issue at hand, managers assign analysts and designate a project manager who manages the analysis and decides the on-demand resource(s) required for the project. The managers from this team help arrange on-demand resource(s). Based on the due diligent analysis, the project manager collects the facts to present the team findings and recommendations for enhancements and implementations of the existing rules and controls or for additional rules and controls.

Business Management: KPI Measurements

Key performance indicators are in common use to manage business growth. Targets are set, and through key performance indicators, growth is measured. The focus here is on secured business operations. The security of business operations directly contributes to business growth. There is a direct relationship between achieving and maintaining a desired level of security and key performance indicators for achieving business growth. Some of the common KPIs for business growth measurements are reducing operational expenses, improving profitability, and improving sales.

The security of business operations is critical for achieving such KPIs for business growth. For illustrative purposes, the key element contributing to the operating expenses is cost of goods sold. This cost depends upon fixed and variable costs. The opportunity here is to control variable costs. The contributing factor is optimizing the operational processes and improving productivity. In the digital age, the critical element impacting productivity is not having the right access at the right time. Having the right access at the right time is the key factor of maintaining secured business operations. This way the related key performance indicator for secured business operations is granting the right access at the right time. The next illustration is for improving sales. Sales depends upon the sales force and the tools available to them for promoting sales, such as for a deal negotiation, for customer relationship management, for checking sales reports, and other such tools. Again, having the right access to the right customers and the right reports at the right time are critical for improving the productivity of the sales force that is critical for growing sales. Then, it is simple math: improved profitability is based on the improved sales and reduced operating expenses. Again, granting the right access at the right time is a key performance indicator for secured business operations. This is not the only key performance indicator for secured business operations. The right access available is critical, however, ensuring that this access cannot be hacked, the tool to which this access granted is protected, and that the information maintained must be prevented from any leakage. The key performance indicators for protecting the sales user credentials from hacking, protecting the tool from hacking, and preventing leakage of business information are all important for securing business operations.

The next critical element about KPI is its measurements. The business management is successful only if KPIs can be measured. The right targets should be set for the key performance indicators, right measurements should be defined for the key performance indicators, and right reporting should be defined to measure status and progress of these indicators. The experience is that businesses are not focusing on defining such key performance indicators and in measuring the progress for achieving and sustaining secured business operations. That is why operational practice is required for KPI Measurements that contributes to the overall success of the business management.

Operations Management: Process Management

As for performing any business activity, a process is required and business process management is a standard operational practice. There are many approaches used, such as Lean Sigma, Six Sigma, Business Process Optimization, and others. To manage secured business operations, the same approaches can be used. Following the lean sigma, five phases – Define, Measure, Analyze, Improve, and Control (DMAIC), the process can be defined and controls can be established.

The security problem in a business operation could be from many reasons, such as access to managed asset(s) used for managing the business operations is not controlled, the information generated for business operations can be leaked, the integrity of information is at risk, the user credentials used to access the information are at risk to be compromised, the firewall in place is not suitable for the federated access for end-to-end business operation execution, and on and on. Using DMAIC, each of these problems or a problem can be defined, the problem potential damage can be quantified, the problem can be analyzed in detail, the solution can be put in place to improve the current situation; and through controls, the solution can be maintained.

For controlling the solution, a process management approach is required. The main thing to emphasize here is that the problem cannot be fully identified just by the Information Security Office or IT, rather, business stake is required to not only fully identify the problem, but to quantify it, analyze it, develop a solution to mitigate the problem, and to properly control it.

Operations Management: Access Control Management

Managing access control is a key achievement for securing business operations. The life-cycle approach is required. The first-time access, ongoing access, and retiring the access, all three phases of life-cycle management, are equally important for maintaining the end-to-end security of business operations. Each business operation end to end performs a number of steps, where each step may require different managed assets, or more than one managed asset is used for executing end-to-end business operations.

Appropriate access needs to be granted to these managed assets for different users. Similarly, each managed asset may be accessing other managed assets for giving business-required capabilities. Each managed asset may be accessed by multiple users and/or each managed asset may be accessed by more than one other managed assets to provide business-required capability. For illustrative purposes, consider a voice service. It is a managed asset. It will require audio, instrument to access audio, means to communicate using voice, audio provisioning from the service provider, billing to a business user department, and few more related managed assets to provide voice capability for a business operation. From a security perspective, it is important that voice is not hacked as it is used for business conversations. All the managed assets described above need restricted access control and protection of voice communications. In brief, a simple capability, such as voice, requires a many-to-many relationship among managed assets as depicted in Figure 4-8.

Figure 4-8. *Many-to-Many Relationship Among Managed Assets for Managing Access Control Management*

This is a simple illustration to convey the point that access control management involved the following:

- Workforce users (could be internal only or both, internal and external) managed assets, represented as digital ids

- Business Application-based managed assets, represented as digital ids

- Infrastructure-based managed assets, represented as digital ids

- Relationship among users and non-user-based managed assets

- Many-to-many-based access control among the managed assets

- Business Processes steps for the business operation

- IT Processes for the business operation

The complexity is added as businesses have many, several thousand to millions of workforce users internally and externally, and several thousand business applications and infrastructure-based managed assets. In addition, currently business transformations for growth and increasing profitability businesses are embracing services transformation, cloud-based business and infrastructure services.

The hope is that the above complexities provide the perspective to understand why access control management is critical for securing business operations. Keep in mind the entire life cycle of access management, involving first-time access, access during hire-to-retire of a workforce user and non-human managed assets, termination of access control, and the need to be strictly controlled to minimize vulnerabilities associated with securing business operations. To securely manage access control, different operational practices are required from Figure 4-3 under Business Management, Operations Management, Risk Management, Compliance Controls, Master Data Management, and Infrastructure Management. In addition, capabilities from the secured business model and all five "P" domains covered in Chapter 3 are required to be used.

The intent here is not to leave access control management as a complex thing to manage; rather, the intent is to justify the criticality of it for securing business operations and provide approaches discussed in other operational practices to manage the life cycle of access control, systematically.

Operations Management: Audit and Monitoring

Audit and monitoring is not only a compliance requirement, but also, it is a critical operational practice for maintaining controls established. As stated in Chapter 1, for cybersecurity a significant proportion of the spending in billion dollars is allocated for fraud and data breach detection with emphasis on Security Analytics, Threat Intelligence, Mobile Security, and Cloud Security. The main purpose of security analytics and threat intelligence is to develop audit and monitoring capabilities for finding potential fraud and data breaches before significant damage is done and to be able to take proactive actions based on the set thresholds. It is like identifying unknown risks for risk management. The focus on mobile and cloud security is mainly due to the fact that growth for businesses is becoming more and more dependent upon business solutions being developed, using cloud-based business services on mobile platforms. These solutions add more vulnerabilities to security if the access controls are not properly managed.

We talked about KPI Measurements as a business management operating practice. One of the key elements in KPI Measurements operating practice is the capability to measure for key performance indicators. Audit and Monitoring provides the means to collect relevant data. The good and commonly used KPI is for managing and controlling unwanted access controls by each workforce user. This is a compliance requirement as well. Companies have deployed a solution based on audit and monitoring to identify a user not accessing a particular tool or service, say for 90 days, and invokes user access after 90 days of the account remaining dormant. This meets compliance requirements, though it adds vulnerability for leaving the access to an account for so long. This is one of the use cases where security analytics and threat intelligence can help determine on a near real-time basis the unwanted access by setting up the right controls and minimizing the associated vulnerabilities by creating near real time to real-time audit and monitoring capabilities. By having an operational practice, it can be a part of your operations DNA to become vigilant by enabling smart audit and monitoring capabilities.

Risk Management: Threat Management

It has become clear that protection from threats is required. That means for securing business operations, threat management operational practice must add value. This value can be added by creating visibility of known threats, creating visibility of the managed assets having threats, understanding of potential risks associated with the known threats, and in prioritizing the known threats. To protect assets, certainly you need to mitigate these threats. In addition to that you should conduct root-cause analysis for mitigating the probability of recurrence of similar threats. This should be in the DNA of your business operational practices. Threat management should not be practiced just when there is a security breach; rather this should be an ongoing operational practice. The overall value of that is the equivalent of increasing the immune system of your body by doing regular exercises.

Risk Management: Vulnerability Management

Vulnerability exposes the operational weakness that poses security risk. It means there is a direct value of strengthening operations by managing vulnerabilities. Healthy operations are like a healthy body. Like a healthy body that allows one to be more productive and creative, healthy operations allow organizations to be more profitable and innovative. Establishing operational practice for managing vulnerabilities means having the capability of registering vulnerabilities, understanding associated threats, understanding associated potential risks, and the capability to reduce or eliminate existing types of vulnerabilities. Having operational practice for vulnerability management means having ongoing associated capabilities to gain sustainable value.

Risk Management: Exception Management

In the context of security, threats, and vulnerabilities, exceptions are business situations that do not fit under threats or vulnerabilities, but pose risks with the potential of producing damages equivalent to the potential damages that can be produced due to threats and vulnerabilities. Due to such potential risks, exception management is equally important, if not more, to vulnerability and threat management.

The value anticipated of exception management is generally more than the value anticipated of vulnerability and threat management. This is due to the fact that by design, exceptions are difficult to register and understand. The risks associated with an exception are extremely difficult to comprehend. Exceptions are not regular and generally misunderstood.

79

Thus, having an operational practice to acknowledge, register, understand, and manage exceptions could be more valuable for securing business operations.

Compliance Controls: Data Security

In the United States, there are industry-specific data security regulations, like HIPAA for the health care industry. This is not like in Europe, where Global Data Protection Regulations (GDPR) are enforced for the entire European Union to all twenty-eight European countries that are part of the EU and to all businesses, regardless of the industries they belong to. The GDPR are applicable outside the EU to any country having EU citizens. The purpose of this book is not to go into the details of individual data security compliance regulations. The point to emphasize here is that to ensure business operations comply with data security regulations, businesses need accountability. Businesses need to have operational practices and not leave it for IT to manage these regulations because these are data-related security requirements. Under the Master Data Management section, there will be more details covered that will assist in managing data security.

Compliance Controls: Segregation of Duties

It is called as separation of duties as well. The straightforward way to understand this is by using an illustrative example – a buyer cannot make payment for the items purchased. In the past, this was controlled merely by giving accounts payable authority to a different person. In today's digital world, that is certainly a fundamental necessary requirement; however, it is not sufficient. It needs to be ensured that the buyer does not have access to an accounts payable automated utility managed asset. If this access control is not managed securely, not only does this vulnerability possess risk to business operations, but it is also noncompliant as per segregation of the duties compliance requirement.

This compliance control is managed by business architecture by setting the right organization structures and creating appropriate roles. However, the automated tools in use require appropriate segregation of duty utilities and access control management to successfully meet the compliance control requirements. Based on our experience, businesses spend the bare minimum to meet compliance needs, but the vulnerabilities created due to not being able to achieve desired access controls pose threats to manage secured business operations. Again, who can manage these access controls? What is required for ensuring appropriate automated utilities are produced so that these access controls can be managed? Business needs to lead this in collaboration with IT.

Master Data Management: Identity Management

We discussed managed asset under the access control management and risk management sections of the secured operating model. These managed assets could be a workforce user (employee, consultant, contractor, supplier, customer, partner), IT infrastructure, process, business products, and service offerings. In short, a managed asset could be a human or non-human. The total number of these assets could be in several thousands, to millions, depending upon your organization size. As these are managed assets, these need to be tracked for securely conducting the business operations. Each asset is granted an identity in digital terms. Each asset has a life cycle as long as it is associated with the organization and contributes for generating value. Each identity is used in one form or another in the other business transaction. It acts as master data for executing a business transaction. At the same time, this is loosely managed by most companies without realizing the implications in securing business operations. To manage identities, master data management treatment is required so that there is a proper data definition for each managed asset type, data integrity and security is maintained for each asset, and appropriate data services are provided for accessing identity data for business transactions.

Master Data Management: Asset Management

By now, it must have become clear that managed assets are critical to run the business. As discussed earlier, the identity management capability manages identity details of these assets for security purposes. As these are business assets, formal asset management is required. Business has distinct functions to manage different classes of assets, for example, HR for employees, contractors and consultants, Customer Service for customers who have relationships with the organization, Manufacturing for product development, Purchasing for vendors, etc. Each of these functions must follow an asset management methodology to manage the life cycle of these assets; the relationship among the assets; the value they generate; the time line of disposition of these assets; and, of course, the risk to quality and integrity.

Master Data Management: Role Management

To maximize return on assets, each managed asset has one or more roles to play in the organization. Based on the given role, an asset is granted access to other managed assets. To keep it simple, let us keep our focus on workforce users- the roles assigned to manage value, competency, and capacity. To maintain a level of separation, ease of management, and avoid unnecessary complexity, the access to various assets is granted to roles rather than directly to users. Roles are master data assigned to each workforce user, maybe one or more than one, for managing access control of managed assets. Figure 4-9 provides how the roles play a master data role for access control management.

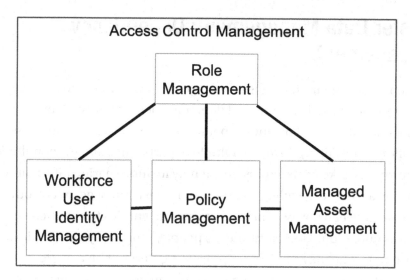

Figure 4-9. *Access Control Management*

For access control management, roles are assigned to a workforce user identity based on policies defined by governance. To manage roles, same master data management principles, Data Definition, Data Integrity, Data Security, Data Services and Data Architecture are required.

Master Data Management: Policy Management

As depicted in Figure 4-9, access control management depends upon policies. These policies are defined and maintained by the governance committee. The policies are defined in collaboration with cross-functional business and IT management who are part of this governance committee. These policies are documented in plain English language for general understanding, yet actionable through access control management systems and procedures. Roles can refer the policy data to enforce access controls for securing business operations. As the policy data is referenced, it needs the same treatment as master data with principles of data definition, data integrity, data security, data services, and data architecture.

Master Data Management: Dependency Management

In Chapter 3 on secured business management, we discussed the type and extent of internal and external dependencies that must be profiled for end-to-end secured business operations. The end-to-end business operations, most likely, involve multiple departments, and even multiple organizations. Like an assembly line, it may include sharing information, executing a workflow, calling someone, sending a message, or any other exchange between any two internal or external entities to complete a business operation. The entity may be people, process, system, or device. For example, one may think order processing starts when a quote is submitted to a customer and converted into an order upon customer acceptance, or when a customer directly places the order online. For the activation to happen, many other activities must have been completed or performed in conjunction for successful order processing. The product pricing and discount(s) were finalized and published by the marketing department. The available shipping methods are explored and decided by the Logistics department. The shipping options are given to potential customers when they are placing an order. The real-time inventory from the warehouse close to the customer's location is needed to ensure timely delivery. It also means warehouse management must plan quantities at different locations based on the research of demand patterns considering various parameters such as seasonality, people demographics, weather, etc. The Legal department sets the policies, terms, and conditions for pricing, shipping, returns that may require customer acknowledgment before accepting an order. Once an online order is submitted, the Fulfillment department needs to take actions for timely packing the orders as per the shipment requirements. The packed product(s) are transferred to Logistics for appropriate shipping and ensuring the customer gets it in a stipulated time agreed in the order submission details. The Customer

Service department may get involved for already shipped product(s) for ensuring full customer satisfaction. Just for order processing, Figure 4-10 shows how many functions and activities might be involved.

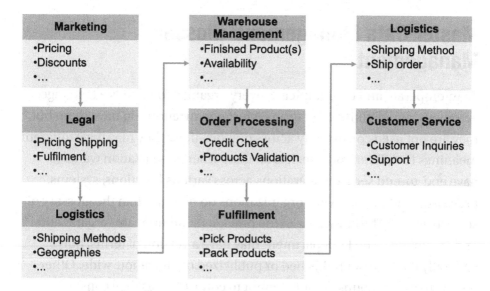

Figure 4-10. *Online Order Processing Inter/Intra Dependencies*

Organizations may use internal resources in terms of people, processes, and systems for all the above functions; or a combination of internal, contracted and outsourced resources for these functions. The above example illustrates that there are always inter/intra dependencies for processing a business operation. The broader and deeper the dependencies, the greater the need to manage the security across the activities for secured operation. It includes securing the back-office or behind-the-scene processes such as procuring the products, manufacturing, customer data, and order data. Therefore, it is important to maintain inter/intra dependencies in a master data form by applying its principles of data definition, data integrity, data security, data services, and data architecture for processing any business operation in an efficient, effective, and secured manner. It is critical to highlight security needs for inter/intra dependencies that can be linked to associated risks and/or vulnerabilities.

Master Data Management: Glossary Management

To interoperate and communicate, every organization needs a language, acronyms, and definitions of terms. Most organizations do have them but they are not used consistently across organization. They may have different meanings to different people. It is an issue when organization wants to have end-to-end secured operations across various functions, systems, processes, and people. Most organizations do not maintain the glossary of security terms. The key words in the previous statement are "organization" and "maintain." The IT department may have a version of terms, but generally they are not published or publicized organization-wide. Other departments or groups do not attempt to contribute, as they consider security an IT responsibility. Where IT department creates a glossary of security terms, there may not be an ongoing effort to maintain it. Why is it important to maintain the glossary? The simple answer is to increase awareness of security, particularly cybersecurity, among the organization's workforce. Without this awareness, it is difficult to keep people informed on security trends and to sustain secured business operations. To start with, use the lists of security terms maintained by the National Initiative for Cybersecurity Careers and Studies or by the National Institute of Standards and Technology. Although the functional groups, such as marketing, engineering, and distribution, may have their own glossary of terms, the security terms are applicable to everyone inside the organization and any external entity with whom there are interdependencies. The glossary must be treated and managed as master data.

Master Data Management: Life-Cycle Management

Every data has a shelf life, and therefore, every data requires life-cycle management. Security data domains, such as identity, asset, role, policy, dependency, and glossary, are no different. As the operating environment or other things change in the organization, an adjustment is needed in security data to reflect the change. Timely and proper adjustments in the definition and attributes ensure ongoing data integrity, data security, data services, and data architecture for secured business operations. For example, a change in the job of a user due to promotions, department change, or for any other reasons may trigger an adjustment in user identity, role, assets, and access controls. If the user profile is not adjusted properly and timely, it could create an unwanted exposure, resulting in potential security threats. When an asset is replaced for any reason, such as end-of-life or new capability requirements, its association with all identities need to remain intact with the replaced asset, so that business operations have minimal to no impact and relevant users can execute their relevant processes securely and with same or better efficiencies. When a role is updated with new or different responsibilities, it may need a change in the things the role can access and perform. In such a life-changing event of the role, there might be a need for identities associated with the original role to continue to perform their operations and do not get any extra access, thus keeping current operations secured. The existing policies may not be sufficient in addressing change in the business conditions, business model or services, requiring a revision and updates to all other assets impacted by the policy. Managing dependencies, particularly interdependencies, can be complicated. For example, let's say your business partner gets access to submit their orders with no export holds, as long as they maintain the embargo with the same countries as your organization. If the partner decides to lift the embargo from one of the countries without getting approval from your organization, submits the order that passes export hold conditions, and the products get shipped to that country, this may pose security threats along with compliance violations for your organization. Ideally, the ability to submit the order to such a country must be adjusted with the life-changing event. Similarly, for the glossary term, if its meaning is expanded or reduced, or a new glossary term is added, it is imperative to timely publicize it so that people are aware and ready in dealing with new cyber threats. To protect business operations, it is very important to keep the workforce informed. It is quite clear that life-cycle management is mandatory for sustaining secured business operations. Master data management is critical for defining and managing the life cycle of each of the security data domains.

Infrastructure Management: Network Management

Network has become an operating system for an organization. It is like veins and arteries in the body for blood to flow across the body. Information is like blood. As the oxygenated blood is important for the functioning of the body, secured information is important for the functioning of the organization. The geographically dispersed organizations are connected using wide area, local area, wireless, virtual private network, and Internet configurations to seamlessly share and access information, and conduct business operations. To prevent leakage of information and protect business operations from hacking, secured network tunnels and firewalls are put in place by network management. To allow only authorized workforce users to access the organization network, only users recognized by Human Resources (HR) are granted access to the organization network. Nowadays, almost every Human Resources department has a step in the hire-to-retire process to grant timely network access at the time of hiring and revoke network access immediately at the time of termination. The timely network access is critical as access to all other managed assets is based on the network access user id. Some organizations have a fairly comprehensive and efficient on-boarding process that may include provisioning of laptop/desktop with network; and access to office services, such as email, calendar, phone, and job-related applications and systems. This is possible only after Human Resources has successfully completed a new hire background check and has given the go-ahead to the Network Management team for establishing user credentials. The user id from these credentials is used for granting access to other core IT and application systems. The technical management of networks is beyond the scope of this book.

Infrastructure Management: Data Center Management

Most of the enterprise information in terms of data and documents, and enterprise services in the form of applications, are hosted in the data center. The data center computational and storage resources may be physically located on the organization's premise, at the location of an outsourced service provider, or in the cloud as Infrastructure-as-a-Service (IaaS) or Platform-as-a-Service (PaaS). Therefore, we are focused on access security rather than physical security. Due to availability of high-speed connectivity at low costs, organizations have consolidated data centers. A few data centers and cloud have made it easier for organizations to secure infrastructure. Companies are using Cloud Access Security Brokerage (CASB) solutions, leveraging servers, storage, routers and switches with built-in security solutions. In spite of using security-aware equipment, the governance continues to be a critical element in ensuring definition and enforcement of security policies. The policies defined for securing the access to data center equipment should not be defined in silo and must be extensible to hosted applications and users. The extensibility helps in reducing points of vulnerabilities, starting with the network-level ids, in the chain of granting and managing access control for hardware, software, and users. Even if the application, such as Excel or email, is running on a user's device, the information whether in files or databases may be stored on the geographical dispersed data centers and situated in a strategic data center location that is provisioned to a business user. Therefore, a securing data center is even more critical in this digital age. The security must not stop at the equipment level and must transcend at a user level for all the relevant managed assets.

Infrastructure Management: Application Management

Applications have been the foundation for enabling business process automation. Organizations prefer buying off-the-shelf applications than building them. Whether buying or building, the applications tend to serve individual business functions, and are hosted on a dedicated infrastructure for the functional organization. Therefore, in this configuration, the security requirements are mostly contained and managed within the application. With the digital transformation, organizations are adopting cloud-based services rather than deploying and maintaining applications in-house. These services tend to interact with other services in the cloud. While there are significant financial and performance benefits of using cloud services, there is an increased level of cyber threats. The service or application management must address the changing nature of the infrastructure, access, and integration. Just like line-of-business application services, cloud-based application management services provide an opportunity to simplify security policies and enforcement methodologies.

Using Secured Operating Model

Each of the twenty-one capabilities in the secured operating model is described as a capability maturity map with five maturity levels. The complete capability maps are available online at securedbusinessops. com website. Organizations can use these maps to assess the current state of these capabilities. Based on the desired state of the secured business model, organizations can determine the required state of secure operating model capabilities. Figure 4-11 illustrates a maturity heat map of a secured operating model.

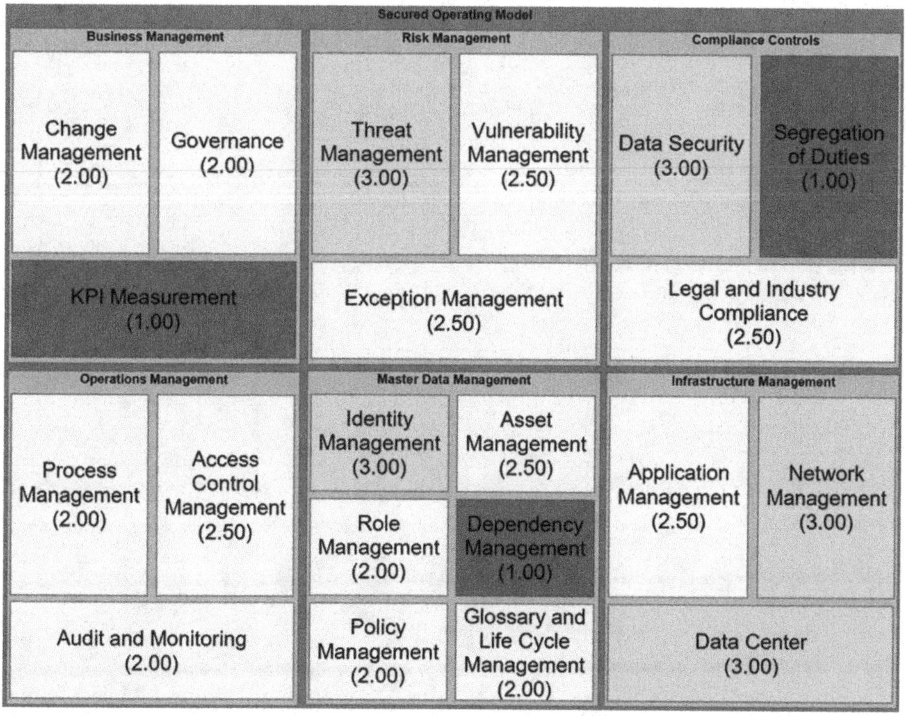

Figure 4-11. *Capability Maturity Heat Map*

Without the business context, it is not fair to say anything low in maturity is not good, and anything in high is excellent. It is possible that organizations might be overinvesting in some areas, underinvesting in others, or just about right based on the business engagement model and business needs defined by the secured business model.

In the next chapter the details will be provided for how to achieve and sustain the desired maturity levels. These maturity levels enable you to maintain the secured operating platform that is necessary for achieving business vision and strategic goals. The structured execution is required once it has determined the desired maturity levels using the template described above.

CHAPTER 5

Secured Management Model

The sustainability is achieved by having a by-design culture of continuous improvement.

Sustaining Secured Business Operations

In previous chapters[1] we laid out the framework to capture the body of knowledge for (a) determining the required risk resilience level for the business using the business engagement model; (b) identifying and developing a road map of secured business capabilities with the secured business model; and (c) assessing, planning, and enabling people, process, information, and technology capabilities with the secured operating model.

In this chapter, the emphasis is on those processes that can be used for achieving and sustaining secured business operations by understanding the top-down requirements of the secured business and operating model.

---

[1]Figure 2-3 and Table 2-2 – determine security resilience level using the business engagement model.
Figure 2-5 – secured business model with 5 Ps and associated 20 capabilities.
Tables 3-2 to 3-6 – appropriate capability maturity models.
Figure 4-3 – secured operating model with 6 process domains and 21 capabilities.

© Neelesh Ajmani and Dinesh Kumar 2017
N. Ajmani and D. Kumar, *Achieving and Sustaining Secured Business Operations*,
https://doi.org/10.1007/978-1-4842-3099-2_5

You can use the body of knowledge in these models to evaluate the current state with goals and objectives, identify the gaps in the existing capabilities, plan the improvements required for achieving the future state, and monitor the progress, as frequently as needed. For achieving and sustaining secured business operations, a security culture is required. This culture ensures that everyone, by design, considers appropriate information security during planning, design, and delivery of any change in business operations or in underlying solutions.

To create a right culture; to have a disciplined approach; to reduce the cost of development, maintenance, and governance; and to create a rhythm of security-conscious change – there is a need of a management model. This chapter focuses on the methodologies and approaches for operationalizing the models and body of knowledge in the framework for ongoing assessment and improvement of information security capabilities across the organization.

Most organizations have established capabilities of portfolio management, change management, value management, solution development, and project management. The management model builds upon these general-purpose organizational capabilities for managing information security. The way quality assurance has become a standard goal in every product/service offering by every organization, around the globe, security assurance for securing business operations would become a de facto standard in every company's operations. The management model can help organizations create the mindset and culture of security by design.

The secured management model is a business-centric, value-oriented process model, addressing the complete life cycle of the security capabilities from envisioning to operations to ongoing improvements for sustainability. Beyond achieving mandatory compliance requirements, security assurance is considered a costly affair without realizing its direct and in some scenarios indirect benefits to grow sales, profitability, brand value among other things, such as improving the quality of operations. To operationalize any process for cost efficiency and broad adoption, it needs a set of practices, a body of knowledge, and an information management solution. The management model incorporates all three design elements for an effective and efficient process.

Components of Secured Management Model

The secured management model is organized into four process domains for holistically achieving and sustaining secure business operations.

1. Assess

2. Plan

3. Improve

4. Manage

Each process domain includes a set of management practices. Figure 5-1 shows these four process domains in a high-level process flow with their respective underpinning practices.

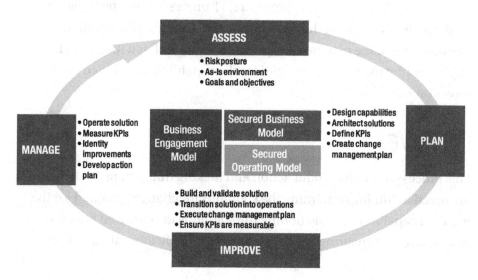

Figure 5-1. *Secured Management Model – Process Domains and Practices*

ASSESS

This process domain can be used for a small context, like for deploying a cloud-based application or for a big context, like overall cloud-based digital transformation. It is used for understanding the change in the business engagement model, evaluating the information security risk based on the changes in the engagement model, understanding the desired goals and objectives, identifying the gaps in the existing capabilities, and deciding for the required capabilities for closing the gaps.

PLAN

This process domain includes practices for architecting capabilities, designing solutions, defining key performance indicators with supporting measurements for required capabilities, and creating a change management plan for the broader adoption of capabilities. The plan may include improvement or change in organizational structure, people skills and readiness, business processes, IT processes, and technologies for properly architecting the capabilities and designing the solutions. The outcome of the plan process provides a well-defined road map for implementing the changes needed for the capabilities identified in the assess process.

IMPROVE

This process domain is about action and making things happen. It includes the practices for implementing the solutions for changes planned for the required capabilities, transitioning the solutions into secured business operations, and ensuring the key performance indicators are measurable.

MANAGE

This process domain includes practices for managing ongoing operations and governance of the capabilities and solutions. Through ongoing monitoring and oversight, new opportunities are identified and start the new cycle of assess, plan, improve, and manage.

There is no doubt that a repeatable process requires a range of best practices. Organizations may have many of these practices. These practices tend to use their own tools, templates, and body of knowledge in a disjointed manner resulting in creating discontinuous and inefficient outcomes. For processes to be sustainable, efficient, and effective, and practices to be adoptable, organizations need a unifying platform for a continuous planning and improvement process. The platform must provide quick and timely access to the information, and must enable the continuity of information, decisions, and activities across the full life cycle of continuous assessment, planning, and monitoring. With the goal of achieving and sustaining secured business operations, the authors not only developed the framework shared in this book, they have also developed a platform to operationalize the framework.

The platform, called CAMP, includes four pillars of capability-driven, business-centric, and outcome-oriented assessment, planning, and ongoing management.

1. **Capability Management**: addressing business and security capability modeling, assessment and planning.

2. **Architecture Management**: addressing enterprise architecture, including business and technology architecture components, standards, dependencies, life cycles, solution patterns, etc., for each capability or business/IT service in the organization.

3. **Maturity Value Management:** addressing strategic planning, road maps, operational and business performance metrics, maturity, and risk assessment.

4. **Portfolio Management:** addressing organization, management, assessment, and planning of various business and IT portfolios such as services, technologies, assets, projects, people, and relevant details.

We live in an environment of constricting budgets with increased focus on value and time to delivery. To continuously deliver high value with ever-shrinking resources, it requires an innovative yet predictable approach to perform various activities related to portfolio building, analysis, planning, and monitoring. CAMP accomplishes this goal without compromising quality and outcomes by effectively combining people, process, information, and technology. Figure 5-2 articulates the overall approached embedded in the CAMP platform.

Defined use cases with methods and
templates leveraging body of knowledge and
platform for proactive and efficient enterprise
portfolio and architecture management

ACCELERATORS with
Organizational Context

BODY OF KNOWLEDGE

VALUE
MANAGEMENT
PLATFORM

Continuous planning,
monitoring and
management of
business and IT
capabilities, services
and technologies

Built-in capability models, best practices,
dependencies and KPIs to fast-track
competency, assessment and planning

Figure 5-2. *About CAMP Platform*

Body of knowledge represents a collective wisdom, experiences, practices, and facts from operations, industry, academia, and subject-matter experts, covering all aspects of enterprise portfolio. As the saying goes, why reinvent the wheel. The body of knowledge includes the models for secured business operations, along with many other sources of information, such as ISO, NIST, ITIL, APQC, Innovation Value Institute, and other relevant sources. The body of knowledge helps to discover "un-knowns" quickly and accelerate their assessment and planning. This can dramatically increase the mutual understanding of the business and IT capabilities.

Value Management Platform is a technology-based service for planning and managing enterprise capabilities and portfolio. It hosts and leverages body of knowledge to plan, transform, monitor, and manage any portfolio initiative from intent to operations. The information in the platform is accessible to various people in the organization to learn and to make their own informed decisions, at any time.

Accelerators represent the art and science of security capability and portfolio management. One can think of accelerators as a collection of engagements, activities or use cases, such as Business and IT Portfolio Assessment, Portfolio Rationalization, Security readiness, Capability Assessment and Planning, Cloud Readiness, Technology Risk Assessment, and Planning, etc. Each accelerator includes a defined body of knowledge configured in the value management platform, methods, and templates.

With body of knowledge, value management platform, and accelerators, organizations can do the following:

1. Develop and maintain the knowledge base

2. Iterate over Assess-Plan-Improve-Manage cycle

3. Empower and enable knowledge transfer

In the next section, we provide additional details on the key management practices in each process domain for achieving and sustaining secured business operations.

Key Management Practices

The secured management model includes 15 key management practices across the four process domains. While the process domains outline the end-to-end life cycle of continuous improvement, the practices within each domain outline the steps and activities involved to achieve top-down and bottom-up alignment with the business engagement model, secured business model, and secured operating model. Every process or practice is actionable in a plug-n-play mode with a set of inputs, actions on the inputs, and produce outcomes. In addition, to facilitate and support an end-to-end continuous improvement methodology, the secured management model provides the flexibility with components for planning and managing security capabilities as part of the overall business and IT portfolio or within the context of a project. As we describe these management practices, we will highlight the key activities and outcomes from the perspective of managing the portfolio and a project.

Assess Process Domain Practices

Any journey, short or long, starts with knowing where you are and where you want to be. Under the Assess process domain, the emphasis is on assessing the risk posture practice along with the standard practices of understanding goals and objectives and the current state of security. Figure 5-3 provides the high-level viewpoint of the Assess process domain with inputs used by its practices to produce relevant outcomes.

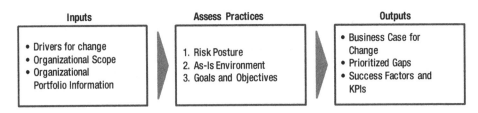

Figure 5-3. *Assess Process Domain*

The inputs to the Assess process domain are the drivers for change, organizational scope, and related portfolio information. In case of portfolio planning, the scope can be all aspects of the organization, whereas in case of a specific project, the drivers and scope are determined by the project. The drivers and scope are not necessarily specific to security capabilities or requirements. The drivers and scope provide the context for understanding risk and identifying required security capabilities.

To evaluate the organizational portfolio and capabilities, organizations need a body of knowledge with a capability maturity model and an assessment framework. In the previous chapters, we have described the business engagement model, secured business model, and secured operating model. These models are used to evaluate various aspects of the organizational scope and organization portfolio of plans, capabilities, processes, people, and technology solutions. These models provide the content, structure, and knowledge for assessing the current state and defining the desired state of the organizational capabilities and competency.

The assessment process is more than finding the gap in the capabilities. The supporting financial business case is required as part of the assessment to justify how by achieving the goals and objectives in a secured manner will produce value and returns on investments. In addition, a value management platform, discussed earlier in this chapter, is used to leverage the body of knowledge and to quickly and consistently assess the organization.

Below is the detailed explanation of each of the three Assess practices.

Assess: Risk Posture

In Chapter 2, we introduced the Business Engagement Model. This model helps organizations identify the extent of access and interaction with people, processes, and systems outside the physical boundary of the organization. Knowing the level of engagement is critical for identifying the acceptable and unacceptable risk exposure, and, in turn, the required information security capabilities. Most businesses have a risk officer at an enterprise level with the focus on business risks. Security risks are generally not under the portfolio of a risk officer. IT departments have information security officer who focuses more with a bottom-up approach and technology perspective to determine and resolve security risks. The security risks pose business risks. The business risk officer, reporting under the business and information security risk officer, reporting under IT, poses risks that can be mitigated by designing the appropriate business organization architecture.

At the start of every initiative, the team should ask the question: In what ways will internal and external people and processes access and interact with systems and information to perform the activities and create the desired outcomes? The risk posture can be assessed by adopting the 5W1H methodology – Why, What, Where, When, Who, and How – for gathering information for documenting in the risk register for resolving risks.

Below are the sample details that can be maintained in this register:

- **Risk** – Name of the risk, for example, customer data theft

- **Description** – Passing unencrypted data in online transactions

- **Source** – Could be a vulnerability, inter/intra dependency, or an exception, for example, customer data vulnerability

- **Business Impact** – High, can impact brand

- **Business Scenario** – Call center issues escalated to customer service managers for resolution

- **Location** – South East Asia

- **Identified By** – Who identified this vulnerability

- **Identified Date** – The date this vulnerability was identified

- **Resolution** – Accept the risk and encrypt the customer data as soon as it is captured

- **Approved By** – Who approved the resolution

- **Approval Date** – The date resolution approved

The risk register should guide the rest of the assessment, planning, and improvement process.

Assess: As-Is Environment

Understand the controls in place for securing business operations. These controls cover all of the compliance in place, policies, and processes in place for managing secured authentication, provisioning, access controls, and authorization management for all types of business operations. Understand the documentation available for these controls. Understand the governance in place for managing the life cycle of such controls. Determine the mix of decision makers' cross-functionally represented in the governance committee. Determine the capabilities in place to manage the as-is environment.

All the items described above can be stored as a body of knowledge in CAMP platform. The as-is environment is dynamic and changes on an ongoing basis. CAMP can be leveraged for keeping the as-is environment current by maintaining it on an ongoing basis. This would enable iterations for Assess-Plan-Improve-Manage and not make this a one-time effort.

Assess: Goals and Objectives

The secured business operations' goals and objectives are defined in the business engagement model, secured business model, and operating model. Here, in the management model, the goals and objectives of the drivers for change, input into the Assess process domain, are understood. These goals and objectives are assessed and the security aspects required are aligned with secured business operations goals and objectives. This alignment is done based on understanding the success factors defined by the business and the existing key performance indicators in use.

Based on the understanding of goals and objectives, risk posture, and the as-is environment details, the future-state environment is visualized. Conduct the detailed analysis to determine the gaps in the existing capabilities and as-is environment to achieve the visualized future state. Determine the gaps in the key performance indicators for achieving the success factors.

Once the outcome of the Assess process domain, which includes the business case, prioritized gaps, and the future-state success factors with KPIs, is produced and finalized, the Plan for achieving and sustaining secured business operations is produced. This plan includes evaluation of the existing portfolio and prioritization of gaps to determine the new projects; programs are required to mitigate these gaps and a road map is developed to sequence these projects and programs.

Plan Process Domain Practices

The Plan process is mainly to develop a design-level plan for the capabilities and changes identified during the assessment process. The assessment outcomes are planned to optimize the improvement efforts. Figure 5-4 provides the high-level view of the inputs, practices, and outputs during the planning phase of the end-to-end continuous improvement process.

Figure 5-4. Plan Process Domain

As success without a plan is not possible, planning security is not a new topic for companies. The question is what is being planned and by whom.

The mandate mostly comes from the office of the Chief Information Security Officer, who reports to the CIO. Are those mandates aligning with business objectives? Are there measurements in place ensuring business success from growth, profitability, and/or a productivity gains perspective? Are such plans ensuring security of business operations? How and who from business resources are involved in making such plans? Are these plans documented and audited? Business is changing constantly, so who is responsible for the life-cycle management of these plans? The point we are making here is that for achieving and maintaining the security of business operations, top-down business alignment is a must, and tight collaboration between IT and cross-functional business functions is required. If the overall mission of the company is to achieve and sustain secured business operations, the planning must include all aspects of the business and technology involved.

The following practices are key for creating a detailed plan for achieving the stated goals and objectives for secured business operations.

Plan: Architect Capabilities

Most organizations jump to the technology solution as soon as a problem or a requirement is identified and approved. Most of us have seen the statistics suggesting over 70% of the projects fail to deliver on the promise. The real issue is in creating the sustainable value by the capabilities enabled by these projects. To generate sustainable value from the new capabilities, before defining the technology solution, focus on architecting the capabilities.

Capabilities describe what business wants to do safely and securely whereas solutions describe how capabilities are enabled at any given time. One can't really identify, let alone design, the right solution without first developing the capability architecture. The architecture scope depends upon the organizational scope and dependencies identified in the assessment phase.

Follow the enterprise architecture approach to architect the enhancements required in the existing capabilities and/or to develop the new capabilities by aligning business architecture with technology architecture. The CAMP platform central repository can be leveraged to maintain these capabilities and associated architect details. This allows you to enable maintaining capabilities architecture details enhancements iteratively that allow tracking the maturity level of capabilities and measure the results for the desired success factors.

Architecting capabilities includes the following outcomes:

- Enterprise architecture details for enhancements to existing capabilities and for new capabilities.

- Identification of business and IT services required to offer these capabilities.

- Identification of projects and programs to develop these capabilities and services.

- Developing high-level plan details in the form of a road map developed for identified projects and programs, based on the architecture interdependencies and the priority of gaps.

Let us understand the details of these outcomes. As there is the misnomer about the enterprise architecture, the outcome produced is not just a technology solution; it covers business architecture, conceptual technical architecture – ensuring alignment between them. The business architecture includes business skill sets required, organization structure changes required, if any, and high-level business requirements to eliminate the gaps through enhanced or new identified capabilities. The architecture maps the business requirements to capabilities, and the conceptual technical architecture provides the functionalities required to meet the business requirements for eliminating the gaps. The business and IT services identification is the expected outcome, but is not generally produced; however, we recommend doing so. The business and IT focus is increasing more toward becoming lean in managing their operations, and shared services is the answer for that, both from the demand and supply perspective: the demand in the form of business services and the supply in the form of IT services. The identified project, programs, and plan costs are estimated at a high level to ensure the costs estimated to generate the business case during the Assess process still hold true. Otherwise, a corrective appropriate action should be taken to architect the capabilities within the estimated costs. Using these outcomes, ensure design details are developed for achieving business success that can be measured based on the key performance indicators.

Plan: Design Solutions

We all recognize that technology is only part of the solution, yet most solution development methodologies are centered on technologies. A good risk management or security solution may be better served by improvement in processes rather than implementation of a new technology solution. The outcomes from architecture capabilities practice are used to develop the following:

- Logical architecture details for the enhancements to the existing capabilities and for new capabilities.

- Shared IT services design by consolidating business services requirements.

- Validation of the identified projects and programs with scope details for capabilities and services.

- Actionable refined plan details for validated projects and programs.

The business logical architecture covers identification of processes required for mitigating the gaps, resources required in the form of numbers and in what business organizations with associated costs detail. The technical logical architecture covers identification of functionalities required to meet business process needs, the number of technical resources required, and in what IT organizations with associated costs detail. The shared IT services design covers the identification of existing IT services and additional services required and mapped to IT services required to meet business services requirements. Based on the scope identification for different projects and programs, the final project and programs are identified with associated scope details. These projects and programs could be for business, IT, or combined for execution together by business and IT team members. The cost details are calculated for each project and program. Based on all these scope details, cost details, and design details, the feasible actionable plan is developed for the execution and improving the existing environment for achieving the future-state environment.

This is all part of designing the solutions required for achieving and sustaining the security of business operations. We suggest that designing solutions produce a solution architecture that should be organized into the following dimensions:

- Services architecture, providing the outward-facing view of the solution in the form of business and technology services and their building blocks.

- Information architecture, addressing the data ownership, classification, sharing, integration, and life-cycle management.

- Security architecture, incorporating appropriate controls, procedures, and measures for secured business operations.

- Technology architecture, analyzing the technology options, and developing the implementation pattern for the selected option.

- Operations architecture, addressing the ongoing operational characteristics, for example, monitoring, business continuity, performance, and support.

The logical next step is to ensure relative key performance indicators (KPIs) are defined for the success factors identified in the business case.

Plan: Define KPIs

Key Performance Indicators are required to measure the effectiveness of the secured business operations in contributions for achieving success factors identified in the business case. What do you mean by effectiveness?

Figure 5-5 identifies business operations components.

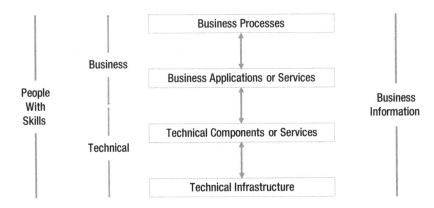

Figure 5-5. *Business Operations Components*

Business operations are comprised of business processes, business applications, or services to execute business processes, technical components or services enabling business applications or services, and supporting technical infrastructure. People with relevant business and technical skills execute these business operations, and generate business information and business value.

The goal is to secure these business operations and be able to measure the effectiveness. Why do we need to make business operations secure? We need to protect these from the following:

- virus, malware, spyware, and other such intrusion elements;

- phishing emails;

- unwanted access control;

- violations in the noncompliance of segregation of duties;

- industry specific noncompliance;

- delays in granting the right access at the right time.

The above reasons all look important, but the effectiveness will be determined based on whether securing the business operations enables achieving the business goals and objectives or not. The business-related key performance indicators are defined during the business planning. The ones that are defined under this secured management model are to measure the effectiveness of improvements made in securing business operations. They have a narrow focus on the drivers for change and identified areas for improvement. Still, these KPIs need to be in alignment with the already defined business KPIs. With the detailed understanding and design of capabilities and solutions, the end-to-end value flow map[2] can be created. The value flow map ensures alignment of KPIs and capabilities.

Organizations may have the capability to measure and monitor lagging indicators, that is, the KPIs that are impacted only after a process has executed, for example, revenue, inventory, cash flow, etc. Organizations find it difficult to measure and monitor leading indicators, that is, the KPIs which provide us insight into the future and enable us to course correct the process for desired outcome. Instrument these leading KPIs into the solution so that they are collected and predictively monitored. We have dedicated Chapter 6 on Security Effectiveness, and there we will further explanation about the associated key performance indicators.

Plan: Change Management

The execution plan is not for just creating new capabilities or enhancing existing capabilities for achieving and maintaining the desired security resilience for your company, but also for ensuring proper adoption and transition into operations of new and enhanced capabilities.

The change management as a capability has been discussed in Chapter 4 under the secured operating model. A capability for change management means that the organization has relevant skills in helping

---

[2]Sample value flow maps are available from The Value Council (vsrcouncil.org).

111

project/program teams create and execute change management plans. From the project management office, a template and resources for creating and executing the change management plan can be offered. Still, this template would need to be tailored to a specific project/program needs perspective.

The main thing to remember is that in the scope of a change management plan, there should be a focus on the following two areas:

1. Increasing the adoption of new/enhanced capabilities,

2. Smooth transition of new/enhanced capabilities into secured business operations.

The change management plan needs to be part of the project plan and it should not be stand alone. The new or enhanced capabilities or services are developed and deployed as part of a project. Their adoption and transition into operations must be the responsibility of a project manager who is accountable for the project.

To summarize, under Plan process domain collectively, the following outcomes are generated with the help of its four management practices to architect capabilities, design solutions, define KPIs, and create change management plan:

- Future-state architecture and design,

- Identified project and program including change management plan details,

- Finalized road map with actionable plan.

Every project makes decisions. The decisions may involve choosing a technology or an architecture approach, changing the priorities and scope of capabilities planned, or assuming things that may have impact on the organization beyond the project. These decisions must be aligned with the overall enterprise governance principles, standards, and policies.

Define and design the capabilities and solutions aligned with the organizational governance framework. Justify exceptions.

These planning practices produce the desired capability and solution architecture, a project plan with cost estimates and change management, and an updated road map incorporating new learnings, decisions, and dependencies. These outcomes are executed with the help of the Improve process domain that we will be explaining next.

Improve Process Domain Practices

The Improve process domain is about implementing what has been planned for improving the current state to the next state of capabilities. Figure 5-6 provides the high-level view of the inputs, practices, and outputs during the improvement or implementation phase of the end-to-end continuous improvement process.

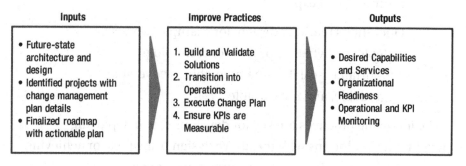

Figure 5-6. *Improve Process Domain*

We assume most organizations have project management and solution delivery disciplines. So, let's focus on practices that can help produce better outcomes from these disciplines, particularly in the context of securing information in business operations. We would like the following key principles added and enforced in development and deployment methods, regardless of organizational scope and nature of the solution:

- Secured by design, that is, ensuring every choice is reviewed and selected and is a best fit for achieving the stated goals and objectives, and does not introduce unacceptable barriers to innovate for the organization.

- Connected by design, that is, no solution can stay in isolation; therefore, even if there are no explicit requirements for interoperability and integration, the solution should not create a constraint and unnecessary complexity for enabling collaborative processes.

- Value by design, that is, any trade-offs during the solution development should be mindful of value promised and expected.

- Operations ready by design, for example, whatever is deployed, whether process or technology, is supportable, scalable, maintainable, recoverable, upgradable, and measurable.

The following practices are key for developing and deploying capabilities and solutions with the above design principles for achieving the stated goals and objectives for secured business operations.

Improve: Build and Validate Solutions

Whether developing a process or a technology solution, we always have choices how we build and deploy. Add objective, measurable criteria for evaluating options and selecting the best fit, balancing current and anticipated needs with by-design principles, organizational constraints, and governance. Having strong project management organizations that can create, manage, and execute a portfolio of program and projects for building and validating the solutions designed and architected using Plan management practices. Once the solutions are built and validated, these need to be offered in a way a business can consume these easily. For consumption, the next important step is to transition these new/enhanced capabilities and services into operations.

Improve: Transition into Operations

In addition to the functional capabilities, there may be a need to manage information produced or consumed by new capabilities for secured operations. The last mile is as important as the first mile. Anticipate what needs to be implemented to manage ongoing operations of the capabilities and solutions and implement them as part of the deployment. The goal is to improve the security of business operations. That is possible only if the new/enhanced security capabilities and services can be transitioned into operations. The project plan should cover plans for how to transition these solutions into operations. This may require adding additional resources having required skill sets to operate. The next step is that the business has visibility of the new/enhanced capabilities and services and can leverage them for securing the business operations. The change management plan is important for making it happen.

Improve: Execute Change Plan

Value is created or realized from new capabilities when individuals change their behavior. Even if the solution automates or eliminates activities, people may continue to perform them. Adopting a change is difficult, as it requires coming out from the comfort zone. Adoption is critical for the success of the project and in achieving the desired outcomes. Execute the change plan developed during the planning phase. This may require appropriate training to increase the awareness and readiness, establishing a community of practice, and monitoring use and experience.

Improve: Ensure KPIs Are Measurable

The key performance indicators are effective when they can be measured. The business process and supporting data need to be available for the measurements. During the Plan phase, when the key performance indicators are defined, the plan must include identified measurements along with the requirements for measuring. The solution must include the required process elements and automation ensuring these measurements can be enabled. Chapter 6 will cover more details with the relevant examples.

Based on the improvements made, the future-state environment is transitioned into operations by producing the following outputs:

- Desired capabilities and services,

- Organization readiness,

- Operational and KPI monitoring.

The new and enhanced capabilities and services are for creating the future-state envisioned based on the architecting capabilities management practice in Plan process domain. The purpose of the future-state environment is to make organization ready for enhancing security capabilities and services offered to secure all business operations. In addition, the operational and KPI monitoring enable the sustainability of the security of the business operations.

Manage Process Domain Practices

The cycle does not end when the solution is transitioned into operations. From the business perspective, it has just begun. During the manage process, the organization starts realizing the return on the investment. Once the capability is achieved, like a secured business operation, there is a need to sustain it. Sustainability requires ongoing monitoring and nurturing of the solutions and capabilities in place, detecting areas of improvements for continuing relevance, and sensing change in business for the next round of opportunities and value.

Figure 5-7 provides the high-level view of the inputs, practices, and outputs during the management process of the end-to-end continuous improvement process.

Figure 5-7. *Manage Process Domain*

Most organizations have been investing in service operations for quite some time with varying degrees of maturity in service monitoring, life-cycle management, and portfolio management. At the same time, many organizations lack effective business process management and value management, resulting in lower than expected benefit realization, high cost of risk management, and increased complexity to maintain secured business operations. Rather than refocusing on what organizations might have, we share and emphasize key practices that organizations need to sustain secured business operations and realize value. The following steps or practices are key for managing and sustaining capabilities and solutions for expected risk resilience and business value.

Manage: Operate Solutions

To secure business operations, the capabilities or services available need to be managed both by business and IT. Remember, business needs to define the operational requirements for security policies, procedures, and business services. Based on these, IT will offer systems' corresponding operational policies, procedures, and IT services. The operational practices need to cover end-to-end life-cycle management of related capabilities and services.

When a new capability or service is put in use, there are business expectations to generate value from it and that value is expected to increase with time.

Figure 5-8 shows the value curve during the life cycle of any capability/ service. As the value starts decreasing, there is a need to enhance the capability/service functionality to optimize the value curve. The other three management practices under manage, "Measure KPIs," "Identify Improvements," and "Develop Action Plan" are leveraged to measure generated value and enhancements required and made for optimizing the value curve of any operational capability and/or service.

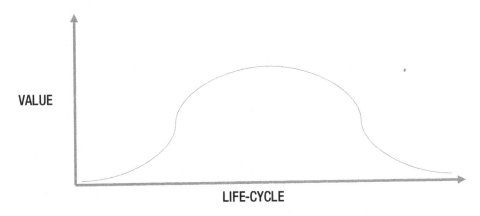

Figure 5-8. *Life-Cycle Management Value Curve*

Manage: Measure KPIs

The key performance indicators are defined in the Plan phase and ensured these are measurable under the Improve phase. These KPIs measurements provide the value generated. It is important to regularly measure these KPIs. Without measurements, it is not possible to ensure whether the operational solutions are valuable or not anymore. As in the Figure 5-8 life-cycle management value curve shows, after reaching the peak value, there is degradation in the generated value by the same solutions. That does not mean that a capability or service has gone bad; rather that means the business conditions have changed and the same capability or service is not as effective in the current business conditions. That leads to the need to identify improvements in the existing solutions.

Without measurements, it is not possible to know or predict the effectiveness of the processes and solutions implemented; their ongoing value to the organization; or when is the right time to retire, replace, or refresh the solutions and decide whether the operational solutions are valuable or not anymore. With measurement data, machine learning, and predictive algorithms, organizations can develop predictive models and improve both strategic and operational planning of security and other capabilities.

Manage: Identify Improvements

The business goals are always to generate maximum value from the solutions used to manage the business operations. These solutions are offered in the form of capabilities and/or services. During the life cycle of any capability or service, when the KPIs reflect the target measurements are not achievable, this means that improvement opportunities need to be identified.

Figure 5-9 shows a pictorial view point of when to focus on improvements for reestablishing target value generation from each capability and/or service. The improvement opportunities can be identified even from the beginning of deploying a capability or a service in production operations. However, the real need to apply improvements is only after the target value expected to be generated is not achievable. The other reason is for continual improvements to improve value generation. The other source for considering improvements in existing capabilities and/or services is when a new driver for a change is identified by business. The identification of improvements is critical, but we all understand that without deploying these improvements, it is a futile exercise. The next logical step is to conduct strategic planning to develop an action plan for deploying these identified improvements.

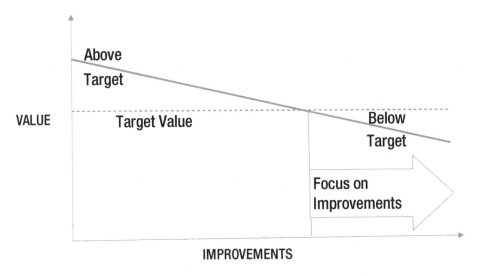

Figure 5-9. *Apply Improvements*

Manage: Develop Action Plan

The implementation of identified improvements is a critical step to improve value generation. The implementation is a costly affair. There are always many capabilities and/or services that would need deployment of identified improvements in the portfolio of security capabilities and/ or services. The budgets are always limited. This gives you the need to prioritize the list of capabilities and/or services as part of strategic planning to develop the action plan. This prioritization is not only required to be done purely based on financial reason. The main criteria to prioritize must always be business damage for not implementing the identified improvements and missing the targeted business value expected.

Once the priority is finalized for each capability or a service in this list, the action plan needs to be developed for implementing the improvements. The Improve: Build and Validate solution management practice is leveraged to execute the developed action plan.

Based on the outputs generated by Manage process domain, the existing capabilities maturity level may need adjustments to address the new vulnerabilities identified in the new drivers for change and to identify improvement areas.

The opportunities for improvements are strategically prioritized in the action plan for further assessment and analysis. The opportunities are evaluated and prioritized for all things business cares about, such as cost, risk, time to deliver, business growth, cash flow, competitiveness, and customer equity.

The strategic action plan is developed for the prioritized list of capabilities.

Conclusion

A project, program and portfolio differ only in organizational scope. The management practices discussed in the secured management model are relevant and applicable to all kinds of projects. For secured business operations, there may be security-specific capability requirements. In many cases, organizations may just need to include security-related assessment and planning in all projects to achieve and sustain secured business operations.

In the last three chapters, we have explained the framework and components of the secured business operations. The business engagement model, secured business model, secured operating model, and secured management model, collectively, provide the body of knowledge for achieving and sustaining secured business operations. Any framework in isolation can lead to overengineering in some areas and underinvesting in others. Particularly in case of security and compliance, fear alone is not good justification. In addition, we have reviewed how this overall framework complements industry frameworks, like NIST 800-171, NIST 800-53, ISO 27001/27002, and many others for achieving and sustaining business operations.

In the next chapter, we explore the model for measuring security effectiveness.

CHAPTER 6

Security Effectiveness

Measuring effectiveness is fundamental for driving adoption and progress toward goals. Customer-centricity is a prerequisite for defining effectiveness.

Current State of Measures

Considering that Information Security is, at best, a governance topic in the boardroom and the accountability is assigned to the IT department, the metrics for measuring security effectiveness, if any, are IT-centric and operational in nature in most organizations. Many of these metrics can be categorized into the following:

1. Process-based measures, for example, how many or what percentage of assets are regularly patched with the latest software updates, how many intrusion or service denial attempts are detected per month.

   IT has processes for managing and monitoring infrastructure security. The related metrics measure communicate the organizational coverage and performance of these processes.

N. Ajmani and D. Kumar, *Achieving and Sustaining Secured Business Operations*,
https://doi.org/10.1007/978-1-4842-3099-2_6

2. Fear and Compliance measures, that is, the number of audit findings, penalties, fear or risk thermometer.

    Organizations, where compliance is a prerequisite to be in the business, have control metrics for monitoring and ensuring compliance. These metrics tend to be a count of required practices, procedures, and policies. Typically, these metrics are used in knowing the existence of the compliance controls, rather than measuring the effectiveness of these controls.

    Security capabilities and investments are primarily justified based on fear. External news and events create a fear of potential financial and nonfinancial damage, causing management to respond. Similarly, many other people, particularly in technology groups, consider every vulnerability a risk that must be avoided or eliminated. Certain fear or vulnerabilities are addressed depending upon how loud they are and who is impacted. Fear and risk can be great motivators for analysis and actions, but they are not sufficient to monitor and measure the effectiveness of security practices.

The above measurement practices are a reflection of how security capabilities are planned and managed, and who in the organization are responsible or are concerned about them. In Chapter 1 and 2, we argued that current practices are not sufficient for achieving and sustaining secured business operations. How do we know what is working? How do we know what must be done? How do we know how effective the remedy or solution is? These questions require additional measures to understand, estimate, and monitor the effectiveness of any security improvements in the organization.

Effectiveness Defined

To make sure we are measuring the right thing, we first need to define what do we mean by the term – effectiveness. When is something effective?

We consider an innovation in medicine to be effective when it eradicates the disease it was targeting. We view our sales strategy or actions to be successful and effective when we acquire new customers without losing money in the process. We accept and adopt a solution that makes us more productive without any friction or extra effort.

Can we say that over $100 billion spent on IT security is effective when cyber attacks continue to cost businesses over $400 billion a year? Do we consider a security control effective if it does not allow employees to work remotely? Is a solution acceptable and effective when it is too expensive to afford?

Based on the analysis of patterns of effective and noneffective actions, we propose the following definition:

Something is effective when it allows achieving an objective or an outcome at an acceptable cost.

An objective or outcome is associated with an operational or strategic goal of anyone in the organization. It can be financial, risk, performance, skill, process improvement, product innovation, or anything else of value. We also live in the world of constraints. We may be able to achieve an objective, but it may come at a very high cost. Effectiveness is like a two-sided coin. For a solution or intervention to be effective, it must enable the desired outcome at a cost the organization can afford. We recognize that people are driven by their own needs. In an organization, individual needs must be aligned with or within the context of the organizational objectives.

What Is An Organization Trying to Achieve?

Every organization or business, regardless of industry, profit/nonprofit, or public/private sector is on the mission to achieve the following:

- Continuously innovate the business or organization.

- Run the business efficiently and predictably.

- Drive the business equity in its brand and culture.

- Keep the business viable and relevant to its constituents.

Figure 6-1 summarizes the typical objectives and drivers of an organization.

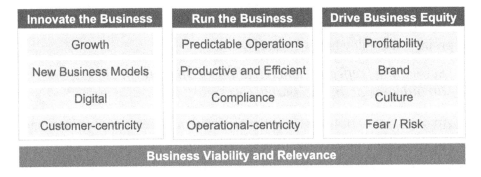

Figure 6-1. *Organizational Objectives*

No organization can stand still and survive on the past successes. Organizations need to continuously innovate products, services, and processes for growth, new business models, digital transformation, or driving customer-centricity. At the same time, organizations cannot ignore what keeps the organization working every day. Everyday activities need to be operationally predictable, efficient, productive, and governance compliant. In addition of being innovative and operationally excellent, organizations are also interested in continuously building its equity.

Equity provides the sustaining power and organizational ability to transform. Anything that improves profitability, builds the brand, creates the desired culture, drives customer's confidence, and avoids unnecessary risk will support the equity objectives. Figure 6-1 list high-level, broad organizational objectives. As we walk down the organizational structure, these objectives should become the outcomes of various decisions and activities performed at each level of the organization.

Anything and everything anyone is doing in an organization, must be aligned and in support of one of these objectives. One side of the effectiveness coin represents producing the desired outcomes as stated or implied by the above objectives. The other side of the effectiveness coin is about the cost of realizing the outcome. So, anything and everything anyone is doing to produce the desired outcome must be at a cost that the organization can afford.

What Is An Acceptable Cost for the Organization?

To know whether a cost of a capability, operation, or solution is acceptable or not, we need to first define what do we consider a cost. Figure 6-2 outlines the key cost elements addressing direct and indirect costs of acquiring, maintaining, and using a capability.

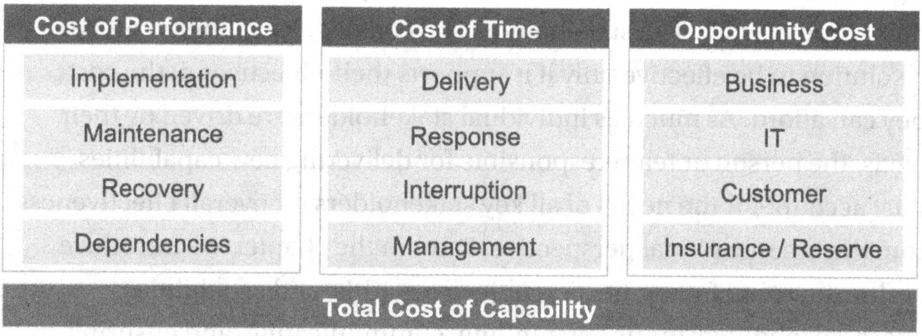

Cost of Performance	Cost of Time	Opportunity Cost
Implementation	Delivery	Business
Maintenance	Response	IT
Recovery	Interruption	Customer
Dependencies	Management	Insurance / Reserve
Total Cost of Capability		

Figure 6-2. *Capability Costs*

The cost of performance includes the cost of implementing, maintaining, and ensuring availability of the capability, process or solution, and underlying dependencies. This is the cost of performing the capability.

The cost of time includes people's time in delivering, responding, dealing with any interruption or disruption, and managing the capability. Some organizations may consider this cost as a soft cost or indirect cost.

The opportunity cost represents the missed opportunities in using the investments for some other purpose. With a finite amount of available time and money, to gain something, something else must be sacrificed. To fully comprehend the total cost of a capability, it must include the impact on the organization from missed opportunities due to the resources consumed by the capability in question.

What Is Effective?

Just like buyers see value differently, the measure and magnitude of effectiveness can be different for various stakeholders. Business managers, business users, IT management, customers, and suppliers may expect different outcomes and may accept different costs. Therefore, the effectiveness must be understood and communicated in the context of a stakeholder. Individual objectives of various stakeholders, although aligned with organizational objectives as in Figure 6-1, are specific to their scope of work. The stakeholders will consider a capability, process, or solution to be effective only if it supports their objectives at the cost they can afford. As much as individual stakeholders are driven by their needs, the person or team responsible for delivering new capabilities must account for the needs of all key stakeholders for overall effectiveness from the organizational perspective. Later in the chapter, we introduce a value flow map for connecting objectives, KPIs, and capabilities across stakeholders for understanding, communicating, and ensuring effectiveness.

Why Are Security Efforts Perceived as Not Effective or Too Expensive?

It would be wrong to suggest that security measures are not effective. Most of the security measures are put in place to avoid the incidents. When security practices detect and remove spams and malware before reaching their destination, thwart unauthorized attempts to access sensitive information, or ensure all devices are up to date in protecting from viruses, they are achieving the desired objectives of avoiding downtime, leakage of proprietary information, and a public relations headache. Like a product warranty, consumers or users don't think of the product quality as the product continues to work. The day there is an issue with the product, they question the quality of the product. Similarly, when most of the security efforts are about avoidance, stakeholders may not think of the value of efforts. They question the cost of these efforts when something harmful gets through the door. A flu vaccine does not guarantee that person will not have the flu, but it does reduce the odds, and in most cases, succeeds in avoiding the flu. Preventive and recovery security efforts may be working but may not be visible to people to realize their effectiveness.

At the same time, there are certain practices that may be creating the perception that security efforts are not effective or too expensive, for example:

- Overengineering the process or solution.

    Engineering minds tend to drive for perfection. Security is one area where it is very hard to reach perfection. Even if possible, achieving 100% prevention may be too expensive. At some point, engineering prevention may cost more than recovery efforts.

- Risk mitigation is the only objective.

  No doubt, fear and risk are the primary drivers for
  safety and security. Security efforts are perceived
  less effective when they take a risk-averse posture
  rather than being risk aware. We tell people to take
  measured risk to achieve bigger rewards. Security
  is no different. Some risks should be acceptable as
  they are manageable.

- Trusting prevention and underinvesting in recovery
  capabilities.

  Of course, prevention is a better cure, but at what
  cost? In most cases, IT is driven by technology
  solutions, hence the bias toward implementing
  preventive solutions. Depending on the total cost
  of the solution, and the frequency and likelihood
  of the incidents, it may be prudent to implement
  appropriate processes and controls for enabling
  quick detection and recovery.

- Measuring and communicating activities, not
  necessarily the outcomes.

  In many cases, security-related metrics are
  focused on operational activities, such as incident
  detection, mean time to fix, patch latency, and
  people awareness and training on security policies.
  These metrics are good for the people performing
  or responsible for the underlying activities;
  however, they are not enough for the people who
  are positively impacted by these activities. If people
  are left to their own interpretation and justification,

most likely they will miss the significance of the metrics to their own activities. Therefore, it is important to relate how improvements in one's activities help improve stakeholders' activities and their outcomes. Use the value flow map, discussed later in this chapter.

Perceived value and effectiveness of security efforts is like an interpretation of a half-filled glass. Whether you look at the glass half full or half empty, business/IT leaders and security professionals need to do a better job in ensuring security efforts are measured and managed for effectiveness in terms of enabling organizational objectives at an acceptable cost.

Principles of Security Effectiveness

Defining, measuring, and communicating security effectiveness is not an art and is not subjective. It simply requires a disciplined approach to identify who the customers are, what do they care about, and how security capabilities can help them achieve what they want at the cost they can afford. To make it practical and repeatable, we have defined three by-design principles for security effectiveness, leveraging the framework we have described in previous chapters.

The three by-design principles are the following:

1.   Start with what and why, not how.

    We all like to solve problems. It is easy to focus and get caught up in the design of the solution. Before we start thinking about how we are going to solve the problem, we should have a clear understanding who the stakeholders are, what metric they are managing or would like to see improve, and what capabilities will enable them. This helps formulate the overall picture with dependencies and value for appropriate and effective solution selection.

Value flow mapping is a visualization technique for building the road map from solution to stakeholder's value. See the next section for details.

2. Do the right things with a customer and business mindset.

    Many times, the solution or process designs are not effective because of the assumptions and ignorance. We assume stakeholders do not want to take risk. We ignore other non-security drivers. Recognizing everyone in the organization has internal or external customers and works toward an organizational mission, to be effective, everyone must put themselves in their customer's shoes and take a holistic view of the customers.

    How do we know and plan what we don't know? We have discussed the Secured Business Operations (SBO) framework in previous chapters. Use the framework to understand, align, and plan security capabilities based on organizational and stakeholders' objectives.

3. Don't just measure what did or didn't happen. Measure the change in capabilities and outcomes.

    Knowing what happened or didn't happen is important for any root-cause analysis or immediate impact of an action. It is critical that we measure change.

New value is created only when there is a change in actions. Measure change in your actions, your customers' actions; and to be extremely effective, change in customers of your customers. Measuring across a three-degree of separation provides the insight into the extent and quality of alignment and effectiveness.

In addition, capability maturity levels are excellent indicators of competency and competitiveness. Use the maturity models included in the framework discussed in this book.

These principles are interrelated and interdependent. The body of knowledge in the Secured Business Operations framework can help build the initial value flow map. The value flow map is used to define the desired state and success factors, and guide the priorities and design options. The following sections in this chapter provide further insight and guidance in driving and ensuring effectiveness of security efforts.

Becoming Effective with Value Flow Map

To be effective in clapping, that is, to be loud and clap longer, we need both hands. In an organization to be effective in producing the desired outcomes, it requires many hands. Resources, activities, and information must be competent, connected, and coordinated for creating outcomes. When an outcome leads to the next outcome, and so on, we have an effective organizational value flow map.

The value flow map was originally introduced by Jack Keen of The Value Council in the book, *Making Technology Investments Profitable*. Since then, we have worked with Jack in refining the value flow map, and applying it to capability-oriented planning.

There are three distinct components in the value flow map, addressing why, what and how.

1. Detect and influence the upstream outcomes. These outcomes are generally stated in the form of financial or operational measures. These measures represent the destinations.

2. Articulate both upstream enabling and their own capabilities. These capabilities represent what is needed, that is, the competency in producing the desired outcomes.

3. Identify underpinning solutions or practices required to improve individual or organizational capabilities. These solutions and practices represent how the organization will build the competency, that is, the ingredients for getting there.

To be predictive in ensuring effectiveness and proactive in communicating value, the value flow map for any organizational, functional, or solution scope must include all three components. Figure 6-3 provides an example of a value flow map for security-related capabilities.

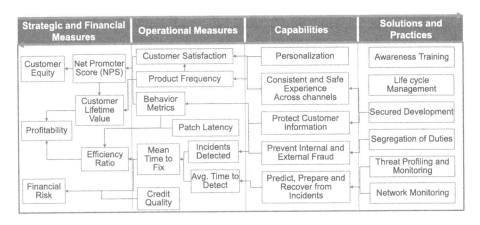

Figure 6-3. *Value Flow Map*

On one hand, depending upon the point of view, the value flow map can be traveled in either direction. On the other hand, building the map is not always linear. As it is about learning, alignment, and ensuring flow, it takes a number of iterations to build the map.

At the top or far left of the map are strategic and financial measures. These are the outcomes that the organization and management leadership are seeking. To reach strategic or financial outcomes, many times improvements in operational measures are required. Therefore, we identify enabling operational measures on the map. The other half of the map defines what and how we could achieve the desired outcomes. The capabilities are the organizational, business, or functional activities required to achieve and maintain operational, financial, or strategic measures. Innovative solutions or practices such as new technologies, new methods, new skills, and new thinking help organizations improve, automate, eliminate, or transform day-to-day activities. In isolation, every solution may be right and worthy of investment. In terms of being relevant and effective, there must be a clear line of sight between measures and solutions. In the value flow map, it is accomplished through capabilities. Once the various organizational measures, enabling capabilities, and solution options are plotted on the map, they are connected to create and communicate the road map to value. Figure 6-4 highlights a road map to value using a value flow map.

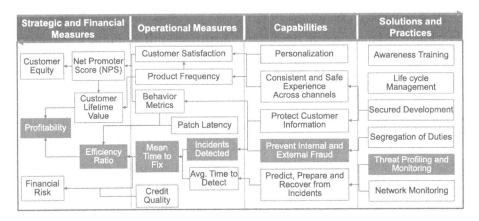

Figure 6-4. *Road Map to Value Using Value Flow Map*

A clear path to value from solution to capabilities to measures, or the other way around, allows everyone in the organization to make the right decisions and avoid chasing shiny objects.

When developing a value flow map, people generally ask, what should be the granularity of measures, capabilities, and solution characteristics? Our typical response is to go wide and deep until you have what you need to know to make an informed decision. The higher the unknowns and complexity, the greater the effort required in developing the value flow map.

If you have customers, internal or external, you can use a value flow map for your services to clearly understand what your customers want to accomplish and how your services can help them. If you are dependent on others, you can use a value flow map to define the requirements and to ensure your suppliers are providing the solution you need. You are effective when value is flowing across the map.

Doing Right with Business Mindset

The great warranty does not compensate for a bad utility. For a product to be useful, it must be fit for its purpose. For it to be effective, it must be useful and available when needed. In the security domain, because of fear, most professionals are risk averse, that is, tend to have the mindset of risk avoidance. No doubt, the risks that can be avoided must be avoided. At the same time, at best, we can only avoid the risks we know. From the business or customer point of view, it is about having a product that meets their needs with an appropriate operational warranty. The warranty means that the product works as expected most of the time, and in case something does go wrong, there are procedures in place to recover quickly and safely. It will be a waste of money to buy flood insurance in a non-flood zone. A B2B manufacturing organization has a different risk profile than a consumer or financial institution. It won't make sense to implement the same policies and solutions in both types of organizations. So, to be effective, security planning needs to be contextual.

There are two ways to become business aware in security capability planning. The conventional way is by asking people in the business. It relies on the assumption that people know what they need and why. In most cases, what they know and plan is based on the past and present issues. People can only plan what they know. Therefore, the conventional approach tends to lead to break-fix or incremental improvements. In the age of crowd sourcing and predictive modeling, there is another approach that uses knowledge models to determine where an organization needs to be, what will it take to get there, and then consult with stakeholders to align, prioritize, and plan. The knowledge-based approach allows us to not assume, but anticipate business needs. With that understanding, we can be effective both in the short and long term in designing and delivering capabilities. In other words, we are managing risk, not avoiding risk.

In previous chapters, we introduced the framework for secured business operations. It starts with the business engagement model. Rather than taking the extreme view by avoiding every possible security risk, business and security professionals can identify the right security risk posture and required resilience level by understanding the extent of interaction the organization has with people and processes inside and outside the organization. Regardless of the scope of the initiative, project, or solution, any security planning and governance can only be productive and effective when the business engagement model is known. See Chapter 2 and Figure 2-3 to understand the level of business engagement and corresponding risk resilience required. Use the business engagement model to determine what kind of business you are today and what you want it to be. The engagement model drives the maturity in underlying business and operational capabilities.

The framework includes a well-organized body of knowledge in the form of capability maturity models, enabling practices, dependencies, and KPIs for assessing and planning business and operational-level capabilities. See Chapters 3 and 4 for details on the secured business model addressing business capabilities and the secured operations model addressing operational capabilities. Leverage these models to quickly learn, anticipate, and assess what business might need and what capabilities are already in place. Share the model and assessment with stakeholders for further alignment, prioritization, and planning.

People are risk averse because of fear of the unknowns. The models help convert unknowns into knowns, thereby enabling people to become risk aware. Addressing business needs while managing security risk is the answer to be effective.

Measuring Change and Outcomes

Change is a leading indicator of value. If you are a solution provider in the value flow map, the change enabled by the solution is the change in capabilities. Therefore, if you want to assess how your efforts or solutions are or might be creating value, monitor the change in business activities caused by adopting the solution. If you are performing a business activity, up-stream change will be the change in business outcomes. So, to know how effective the business activities or capabilities are, measure and monitor the expected outcomes.

The value flow map provides the continuum from solution to capabilities to outcomes. The value contribution or effectiveness can be measured and articulated by tracing the flow map.

Key Measures for Security Effectiveness

Ultimately, the security practices are effective when they produce the expected outcomes for the stakeholders. Therefore, the ultimate measures for effectiveness are the outward measures, that is, the performance measures of the stakeholders. Typically, the outward measures have two or more degrees of separation from where security practices are performed. It is not always easy or it may take some time to see the impact on these outward measures. Therefore, we must have inward measures or leading indicators, measuring the extent and performance of the security practices and their impact on the immediate customers or users of these practices. The following Table 6-1 provides guidance on potential measures.

Table 6-1. *Measures for Security Effectiveness*

Type	Category	Measures
Outward Measures	Value Enablement	• Introduction of new or improved business capabilities (innovation). • Business cost reduction or avoidance (run the business efficiently and competitively). • Market position, for example, brand value (business equity).
	Compliance	Criteria as specified by applicable compliance framework.
Inward Measures	Capabilities	Maturity Level of various business and operational capabilities defined in secured business model and secured operating model.
	Practice Performance	• For each practice, measure its efficiency in terms of time, effort, and quality of output. • Capability or practice specific performance measures. Each practice has one or more objectives, defined by one or more measures, that is, people trained on security policies, patch latency, spams detected and removed.
	Risk Management	• Indicators how well are we managing risk, for example, exceptions to the governance policies. • Execution of key controls, for example, segregation of duties, rights-enabled documents.

The above table is not an exhaustive list of measures. The framework for secured business operations includes relevant KPIs for specific capabilities in the secured business model and secured operating model. The value flow map, discussed earlier in this chapter, is an effective way for identifying and measuring relevant measures for the organization.

Measure to Manage

In previous chapters we shared the framework and body of knowledge for planning, designing, and managing secured business operations. In this chapter, we discussed how organizations, particularly security professionals, can articulate and measure the effectiveness of capabilities and practices, thus avoiding overengineering or barriers to business innovation. The framework with a clear set of measures enables organization to achieve and sustain secured business operations while continuously transforming the organization to meet customer expectations. In the next and final chapter, we share use cases and approaches for making it real for your organization.

CHAPTER 7

Making It Real

The journey of a thousand miles starts with one step at time. To keep going, keep taking the next step, however small it may be.

—Chinese philosopher Laozi

What Have We Learned?

Seamless connectivity, personalized products and services, real-time collaboration and transactions, automation, predictive insight and actions, use of public or shared infrastructure – these are some of the transformations many organizations are exploiting or exploring to be competitive, productive, and responsive. No doubt, these transformations are making organizations open and easy to do business with. These transformations are also making organizations more vulnerable and exposed to information thefts and cybercrime threats. If the security efforts in your organizations are not producing the desired results or increasingly becoming cost prohibitive, something must change the way the organization plans and manages security capabilities. In previous chapters, we have discussed the potential changes required and shared the framework for holistic and proactive management for secured business operations. In this chapter, we are summarizing the key takeaways and share a few use cases.

© Neelesh Ajmani and Dinesh Kumar 2017
N. Ajmani and D. Kumar, *Achieving and Sustaining Secured Business Operations*,
https://doi.org/10.1007/978-1-4842-3099-2_7

1. *Security is a business issue, not only a technology issue. Therefore, business management can't afford to delegate planning and risk management to technology teams.*

   Whenever there is a security breach or incident, it becomes a business issue and priority. So, why does business management take a passive approach for planning and managing information security? Just like quality and safety, information security can't be achieved just with better technology. It is an organizational capability and therefore it must be planned and managed along with other business capabilities.

2. *Fear and compliance are not the way to address, plan, and fund security capabilities.*

   It is understandable that compliance may be a prerequisite for the business. Compliance requirements are there for reasons. Addressing the underlying reasons should be the driver for planning security capabilities. Organization will not only achieve compliance but also create an empowered, security-aware culture. Addressing the compliance requirements without focusing on the underlying reasons will only ensure a forced and compliant mindset.

   The planning based on fear of the unknown generally results in overengineering or overspending – we either stop thinking rationally or end up spending an unreasonable amount of money on something. Better understanding of risk, impact, holistic view of the required capabilities, and solution options reduce the degree of unknowns and the magnitude of the fear. Use the capability models and value flow maps to translate unknowns into knowns and fund the right capabilities and solutions.

3. *Security is a competitive advantage, not just a cost of doing business.*

    Something is a competitive advantage if it is difficult for the competition to imitate. Something is required for competitive parity when others have or can acquire that capability. Industry is spending lots of money with an average return on investment at best. Most business leaders are concerned about the security capabilities and cost. It means it has not been easy for organizations to achieve and sustain secured business operations with the level of investments they made. The organizations, which have been able to advance maturity in organizational capabilities, such as quality, seamless ecosystem, service orientation, digital, and others, have created and sustained competitive differentiation. Security is one of the illusive organizational capabilities, which everyone wants, but only a few have been able to realize in alignment with their level of business operating model. Current practices in security planning and management continue to promote security as cost of doing business. We believe the framework for secured business operations, discussed in previous chapters, provides organizations the knowledge and tools necessary for embedding security in their operations and offerings for a sustainable competitive advantage.

4. ***In many cases, processes are more effective than technologies in preventing and recovering from incidents.***

One cannot achieve a high quality or safety just by acquiring better tools, machinery, or instructions. In many cases, it also requires improvement in processes and skills. In fact, we have learned that many times, the processes are more effective, less costly, and disruptive than using technologies to solve a business problem. Security is no different. Organizations can't afford to manage security risk with one tool, that is, technologies. Organizations may reduce the number of incidents with the use of technologies, but when an incident does happen, it is the processes and people skills that allow organizations to avoid customer distrust and negative publicity. Therefore, any capability planning must take a holistic view of people, process, information, and technologies, to determine the appropriate and effective approach to address risk. The capability assessment using the secured business model and secured operating model exposes the gap and opportunity in leveraging people and processes for improving security posture.

5. *Avoid over-or underinvesting by aligning investments to business engagement level.*

Security is not a "one size fits all" solution. Information risk is proportional to type and level of access and interactions outside the organization's direct control, that is, the extent of business engagement with customers, partners, and employees. The organization that is open for business by providing remote access to its employees and sharing information in real time with customers and partners is going to be more vulnerable than the organization that does not provide remote access. The scope and investment in security capabilities must be consistent with the risk level carried by the organization based on its business engagement model. If an organization doesn't know its engagement level, most likely, it is either overinvesting or underinvesting in security capabilities. The business engagement model[1] articulates four distinct types of engagements or interactions, starting with a self-contained organization with no outside access and collaboration to a digital organization. See Table 2-1 for details. It is a very quick exercise. Don't postpone it.

---

[1]Business Engagement Model is explained in Chapter 2.

147

6. ***Assess and manage capabilities for achieving and sustaining secured business operations.***

   Security is not something you implement and forget. With continuous change in business, people, information, technologies, customer expectations, or relationships, organizations cannot just deploy a solution, implement a process, or establish a policy and expect to mitigate the risks forever. Did you ever notice that military leaders always talk about capabilities to accomplish the mission? They don't start the conversation with processes, ammunition, fighter jets, etc. They are focused on acquiring and maintaining the capability to fight any mission now and in the future. They understand the dependencies and make sure they have what is needed to sustain the capability. We propose the same mindset and approach for achieving and sustaining the mission of secured business operations. We also recognize that people can only plan what they know. Therefore, we created a body of knowledge and capability management framework for secured business operations. In Chapter 3, we described the secured business model for business to understand and identify the capabilities and maturity in those capabilities they need across 5 Ps – Prevent, Protect, People, Policy, and Profile. In Chapter 4, we focused on the underlying operational capabilities organized as the secured operating model. Together, the secured business model and secured operating model provides organizations to embrace the capability mindset and start assessing and planning secured business operations.

7. ***Embed security in every role, process and project planning, by design.***

Just like customer-centricity, quality or cost-efficiency, security must be planned and planted in every other planning and design activities. Without the security-conscious culture, risk management is too expensive and porous to be effective and sustainable. Organizations can start by asking a few simple questions during planning, approval, and oversight activities in making sure the teams are considering security implications of whatever they are doing or proposing. For example, if the role, process, or project changes the way or the extent of interactions with other people and processes, we need to ask how we are preventing and protecting unauthorized access to sensitive information. To create a security mindset, we introduced a secured management model in Chapter 5. The model provides the structure and steps for incorporating security assurance through the assess-plan-improve-manage phases of any initiative or change execution. In every planning and design effort, people have choices. Organizations can avoid rework and avoidable risk by ensuring that people are making the right choices with security in mind.

8. ***Measure effectiveness, not just operational or process metrics.***

Activity-based measurements are primarily good at measuring process efficiency and operations, such as time and effort involved, number of people trained, or number of viruses detected. These measures are required but not sufficient to comprehend overall effectiveness and value of the security-related activities and solutions. The security efforts should not be just about prevention and protection; they should also enable business innovation and transformation. To clearly articulate, measure and communicate the effectiveness of security capabilities; it requires identifying and measuring up-stream activities and outcomes. On the flip side, the same measures can also help in identifying and prioritizing the required security capabilities. Organizations may want to use value flow maps, described in Chapter 6, for linking security solutions with outcomes to measure and ensure their effectiveness.

What Has Been Done?

The framework for secured business operations is the result of many years of direct work with various organizations across industries and sectors, and the observations on success and challenges with many existing practices. Looking back, we can summarize our journey in three steps.

1. Building the various aspects of the framework as we were delivering the engagements.

2. Formalizing the body of knowledge with a value management platform, and applying the framework as designed.

3. Sharing the framework.

Although there have been variations in the starting point and road map for driving security capabilities and culture, broadly speaking, the use cases can be categorized into three areas.

- Using the body of knowledge in the framework, for example, the business engagement model and capability maturity models to enhance existing methods and templates for better outcomes.

- Performing portfolio assessment and planning in support of organization initiatives, such as merger and acquisitions, digital transformation, leveraging the cloud services, and strategic or budget planning.

- Driving and ensuring appropriate risk posture and security governance in business and IT projects.

The following four use cases show how organizations started addressing the challenges and opportunities at the time. All these organizations understood and expected the broader change in the way they think, plan. and manage security capabilities. They also realized that it will take multiple years as they work on initiatives and opportunities over time across the organization.

1. A technology manufacturing global Fortune 500 company, improving the security posture of its products, services, and operations.

2. One of the top health-care services providers in the United States, expanding its operations globally.

3. A national service provider with an extensive partner network, going through a merger with another service provider.

4. A hospital network with distributed facilities, evaluating and planning information and infrastructure services for improving cost, care, and communication.

Technology Manufacturing Company Open for Business

The company has been using an Internet commerce platform with its customers, partners, and suppliers. The company was growing through mergers and acquisitions. As the commerce platform was becoming central to the business strategy and operations, the organization was challenged with scalability, adaptability, and information security.

In spite of the commerce platform being critical to the business, like most technology-based issues, the problem and therefore solution was originally left up to the technology teams to address. The bottom-up approach led to plumbing gaps and adding infrastructure resources. No one was satisfied with the outcomes. The organization decided to take a top-down approach, establishing it as a business-driven initiative with cross-functional leadership sponsorship and support.

Using the business engagement model, it was quickly determined and agreed by the leadership team that the organization wants to be a connected business (level 4) with the eventual goal to be a digital business (level 5). The current practices and solution were operating at level 3, that is, designed for business-to-business operations. Knowing the engagement level, management started asking the question of what do we need to get there. It was no longer a technology issue. The functional, operational, and risk resilience capabilities must support the organization to be a connected business.

Recognizing that organization needed to be at level 4 in the capability model, at a minimum, the key stakeholders across business functions such as manufacturing, sales and marketing, customer service, legal, HR, finance, and IT were surveyed for determining organizational priorities, focusing on the five Ps: Prevent, Protect, Policy, Profile, and People aspects of the secured business model. A risk register and 3-year road map were developed, initially focusing on the capabilities needed for the internal workforce.

Identity and access management (IAM) was one of the first rounds of operational capabilities to be further analyzed and developed. Using the IAM capability maturity model from the secured operating model, the current and target states were defined, and the underlying dependencies and practices were identified. A project plan was developed, addressing required capabilities and dependencies.

As the program progressed through the phases, additional capabilities such as policy management, role management, and resource management were addressed.

Overall, it took over three years in addressing people, process, policies, platforms, and performance capabilities for secured, scalable, and flexible business operations. The top-down planning and iterative execution ensured alignment and value delivery.

Since then, the organization has added security as a track in every project and as part of governance, ensuring every delivered product and service is designed for secured business operations.

Leading Health-Care Provider Expanding Globally

A U.S.-based leading health-care provider wanted to extend its reach by collaborating with other providers and research organizations around the world. It also wanted to make sure patient privacy is preserved and regulatory requirements such as HIPAA and PCI are met while it communicates and connects with other organizations.

The organization conducted a holistic assessment of business and technical capabilities needed to support the collaborative yet secured environment. The top-down, process capability assessment focused on business needs, business operations, and security risks. The bottom-up, technical capability assessment evaluated the current state of various management, operational, and infrastructure practices and technology solutions. The assessment included identification of the following:

- Outdated network infrastructure elements, unsuitable to manage cybersecurity threats.

- Web-based applications with insufficient security architecture.

- Policies and procedures for end-to-end access control and life-cycle management.

The organization used components of the secured business operations framework to assess, and more importantly, to establish a target state and developed a multiyear road map.

A Service Provider Merging with Another Service Provider

A membership-based consumer service provider has been expanding its member base through value-add information services and acquisition of other service providers. In the past, like most M&A, the portfolio rationalization and consolidation activities were primarily focused on application and infrastructure technologies. Information security capabilities were not considered during the portfolio rationalization, resulting in many surprises and unnecessary remediation costs.

The organization decided to improve its due diligence and portfolio rationalization process by including security assessment of the business and IT processes, and technology portfolio. It used the maturity model of twenty-one capabilities in the secured operating model to assess the organizational and operational capabilities of the acquired organization. Using the 5 Ps of the secured business model, it developed criteria for assessing the security posture of each application under consideration for rationalization. The enhanced approach has helped the organization with better understanding of respective strengths and weaknesses of their security capabilities. The organization is able to make informed decisions to prioritize and plan based on cost, risk and value to avoid budget surprises.

A Hospital Network Optimizing Cost and Maximizing Care

The hospital network embarked on the digital transformation with electronic medical records, communication, and collaboration with patients and doctors, and shared services across the network. The organization was also concerned about increasing the cost and health of the infrastructure supporting the network.

The Chief Technology Officer (CTO), a business leader reporting to the CEO, initiated overall assessment of core enterprise services, including communication and collaboration, process and data integration, information security, directory, and networking services. To be objective and comprehensive, and at the same time efficient, the team leveraged available capability models such as the secured operating model, infrastructure optimization and service management, and developed a few maturity models where they were not readily available. The consumer and provider of services across the organization were interviewed using the models. Based on the gap identified and feedback, a road map with the business case was developed. As the organization moved forward with the plan, progress was monitored and reported against the maturity model and expected outcomes.

What Can You Do?

By now, we are confident that you do realize something must change the way the organization plans and manages information security capabilities, and the framework for secured business operations can be the recipe to make that change happen.

A successful adoption and value realization requires overcoming internal barriers and working around the constraints. So, what you can do is think proactively about it and address your own organization barriers and constraints. In Table 7-1, we have identified barriers we have observed and potential actions one can take.

Table 7-1. *Organizational Barriers and Constraints*

Barrier or Constraint	How do you know? (indicators)	What can you do? (actions)
Risk-averse culture	• Failure is not an option (penalties for taking risk). • Justification based on fear. • Question asked - What is in it for me? • Avoiding external dependencies in projects or processes.	• Translate unknowns into knowns with capability models. • Identify value for each stakeholder using value flow maps. • Develop success stories.
Lack of business ownership and accountability	• Chief Security Officer (CSO) reports to CIO. • Business people think security is in their way of achieving success. • Business is concerned about IT security cost.	• Show linkage between the outcomes and capabilities using business engagement and secured business models. • Measure and communicate effectiveness of security efforts.

(continued)

Table 7-1. (*continued*)

Barrier or Constraint	How do you know? (indicators)	What can you do? (actions)
Appetite for change	• Too many initiatives. • Short attention span and change fatigue (another change before previous change can take hold).	• Develop multiyear road map with frequent value milestones. • Start anywhere, go everywhere by leveraging existing initiatives.
Organizational structure	• Independent business units. • Lack of effective governance structure or process.	• People are driven by their needs – articulate value in stakeholder's context. • Think global, act local by aligning with business unit specific priorities.
Short-term mindset	• Annual budget planning, not necessarily strategic planning. • Expecting return on investments within the budget year. • Incremental change.	• Begin with the end in mind. Plan and deliver value in short term with long-term view. • Present alternatives that may include status quo, incremental, and transformative approaches.

Approach for Adopting and Operationalizing the Framework

We don't suggest introducing a framework for the sake of a framework. It must address the need of the organization. You may need to adopt and integrate parts of the framework. You must also plan on operationalizing the framework beyond the initial awareness and capability assessment. To help organizations adopt and operationalize the framework quickly, you can use CAMP,[2] a cloud-based software as a service with ability to assess, plan, and manage capabilities and generate value using the secured business operations framework.

Some people are motivated to adopt the framework when they see what it can do. We invite you to contact us. We have preconfigured an online platform with a complete body of knowledge to quickly assess the organizational capabilities. The assessment may provide an interesting insight to jumpstart the journey toward achieving and sustaining secured business operations.

---

[2]For more information, see www.mitovia.com/camp.

Index

A

Accelerators, 99

Access control management, 83
   end-to-end security, 75
   first-time access, 77
   managed assets, 75
   practices, 75–76
   many-to-many
      relationship, 75–76
   voice service, 75 (*See also*
      Operations management)

Adopting and operationalizing
      framework, 158

Application management
   practices, 90. *See also*
      Infrastructure
      management

Architecture management, 97

Assess and manage
      capabilities, 148

Assess process domain, 96
   environment, 103
   goals and objectives, 104
   inputs, 100–101, 104–105
   outputs, 104–105
   risk posture, 101–103

Asset management
   practices, 82. *See also* Master
      data management

Audit and monitoring
   practices, 77. *See also*
      Operations management

Automation, 5

B

B2B engagement model, 27–30

Big data, 2

Body of knowledge, 99

Bridge between capabilities and
      solutions, 36, 47
   secured business model, 36

Business engagement
      levels, 15–16, 92
   aligning investments, 147
   vs. risk resilience levels, 17, 45

Business management, 54
   capability building blocks, 55
      change management, 69–70
      governance, 70 (*see also*
      Governance)
      KPI measurements, 73 (*see
      also* KPI measurements)

Get the eBook for only $5!

Why limit yourself?

With most of our titles available in both PDF and ePUB format, you can access your content wherever and however you wish—on your PC, phone, tablet, or reader.

Since you've purchased this print book, we are happy to offer you the eBook for just $5.

To learn more, go to http://www.apress.com/companion or contact support@apress.com.

Apress®

Printed in the United States
By Bookmasters